Lessons of Life

Wisdom from an Ageless Generation

by

Writers Group of Leisure World

Copyright © 2018 by Writers Group of Leisure World

All rights reserved

Paperback IBSN: 978-1-7346579-2-0

eBook IBSN: 978-1-7346579-3-7

Library of Congress Control Number: 2021904092

Contact an author at WritersGroupofLW@gmail.com

Cover design by Sarna Marcus
<www.sarnamarcus.com>

Printed in the United States of America

TABLE OF CONTENTS

INTRODUCTION ix

CHAPTER 1 - An Extraordinary Life by Lee Hardy 1
How I Came to Be ♦ A Teen's War ♦ Think (of) It! ♦ "Run" ♦ Memories ♦ Texas Thanksgiving Family Dinner ♦ Great Grandson, Havie, Xavier, X Man, Whatever Name You Choose ♦ Just Do It ♦ By Gosh, A Seusse-ical Slosh ♦ Snow, Oh No! ♦ Snowy Morn ♦ Featherston Memories ♦ Geessaltafreedenhaven ♦ Fragile

CHAPTER 2 - Love Poems by Danuta Montorfano 15
My Mother's Garden ♦ Edelweiss in Exile ♦ Sleepy Town II (Blizzard of 2016) ♦ Lone Walker ♦ Afternoon in Como ♦ The Boulevard of Yellow Flowers ♦ Separate Beds ♦ Autumn Day ♦ About Postponing ♦ Gifts from Nature ♦ Enjoy What's Left or So Little Time

CHAPTER 3 - Poems of Love by Carlos Montorfano 25
Noses, Noses ♦ Me! ♦ A Red Rose? ♦ Thanks, Mother Nature or Compensation ♦ I am Full of Empty Spaces ♦ Middle Age Exercise or Why Suffer? ♦ The Descent of Man ♦ Monosyllabic ♦ Memory ♦ My Music ♦ Nobody is Perfect or The Secret of Life ♦ I am Obvious ♦ Music to My Ears ♦ Woolgathering

CHAPTER 4 - What's It All About by Gladys Blank 33
Remembering the Good Times ♦ At Sea ♦ Ides of March ♦ Book Club

CHAPTER 5 - Life by Grace Cooper   41

Big Little Things ♦ Four ♦ T'is Of Thee ♦ Night ♦ The Day After Tomorrow ♦ Misty ♦ Three A. M. ♦ Knit One ♦ Night Shadows ♦ Winter Love ♦ Facade

CHAPTER 6 - A Few Captured Thoughts by Radha Pillai   49

A Wishful Thinking ♦ Big Old Banyan Tree ♦ Earth's Lament ♦ Ethics, Morality, Civics, etc ♦ If ♦ Live the Moment ♦ Nothing at All ♦ Spring ♦ Nuggets from My Memory Chest ♦ The Human Ingenuity ♦ The Sacred River ♦ You Are What You Eat ♦ Fate ♦ Rock Creek Trail

CHAPTER 7 - World Traveler by Jane Hawes   67

A Bushy Tale ♦ Pillsbury Dough Boy ♦ Remembering the Innocence ♦ Miss-Haps in Japan ♦ Snap Shots ♦ The Chinese Experience ♦ Mayo Wan Te ♦ Sahwadee ♦ Camping ♦ Island on the Equator ♦ Animal House ♦ Mr. Kim ♦ Kowtow Kowloon - "Traditional Kowloon" ♦ Only Your Own Teeth Need Apply ♦ The Secret Attacker - Lyme Disease ♦ Guardians of the House ♦ Quack! Quack!

CHAPTER 8 - A Student for Life by Marion Bedell   101

The Test ♦ Flight from Life - Part Time ♦ Love? or Not! ♦ Secrets ♦ The Decorator ♦ Red Roses

CHAPTER 9 - Artscape by Denise Barker   111

The Bronx ♦ Artscape ♦ Waiting for Rain ♦ Magoo: a Dog Story ♦ Pop ♦ The Stoop

CHAPTER 10 - My Amazing Life by Joanie Friedlander   117
Gun Totin' Cowboy ♦ Good Vibrations ♦ Awkward First Dates ♦ Innocence Lost and Found ♦ After My Divorce

CHAPTER 11 - David by Viola Stendardi   125

CHAPTER 12 - Memoir Essays by Verna Denny   129
75 Steps ♦ Hope and Honor on Mother's Day

CHAPTER 13 - Deer Tales by Woody Shields   137
Gullible Hunter ♦ Is Deer Hunting Really Better than Sex? ♦ Hunter-Employer Relationships ♦ Deer Camp Experience

CHAPTER 14 - Life in DC by Anne Doherty Rinn   149
What It Means to be a Washingtonian ♦ To Be or Not To Be Prejudiced ♦ The 1930s In DC ♦ A Child's Summer in DC before Air Conditioning ♦ It Was the 50s and Early 60s ♦ Past, Present, and Future ♦ Our Bamboo ♦ We Human Beings ♦ Out of the Mouths of Babes ♦ God's Entertainment Box ♦ An Irish Mist

CHAPTER 15 - Reality and Beyond by Bobbie Troy   163
We Need to Believe ♦ I Speak to You ♦ Dear Diane ♦ The Door of Life ♦ Reality Heals Itself ♦ Surviving Auschwitz ♦ Beyond Tomorrow ♦ Answers ♦ The Greatest Lesson ♦ Layers of Time ♦ The Fallen ♦ She: Losing the Plot ♦ My Mind Is Free ♦ Emptiness

*To all those who nurtured
the birth and growth of our
"Writers Group of Leisure World"
with special recognition to Jean Featherston
and Mary Zenchoff
the two previous presidents
who are no longer with us.
And
to our dear friend, Carlos Montorfano
who passed away while
we were compiling this book.*

INTRODUCTION

Our Writers Group of Leisure World is blessed with diverse members whose talents cover many walks of life. Our writers include published authors, renowned professors, and people like me with little previous writing experience. We spin our tales, poems, essays and opinion pieces for our readings, appreciating each unique contribution. In this way, we have woven our lives together with our written words into a delightful social community, eliciting emotions from laughter to tears. What a wonderful friendship we have created!

With great admiration and humility for my fellow writers, I am very pleased to present to you our book, "Lessons of Life, Wisdom from an Ageless Generation" on behalf of the Writers Group of Leisure World Maryland.

May the words within lighten your spirit with humor and joy, move your sensibilities to positive action, open your mind to new perspectives, and fill your heart with love.

Sincerely,

Radha Pillai
President, Writers Group of Leisure World
Silver Spring, Maryland

♦ ♦ ♦ ♦ ♦

CHAPTER 1

An Extraordinary Life

By Lee Hardy

How I Came to Be

Sometimes I think I have led an extraordinary life. Other times, I'm sure of it. Having survived multiple abortion attempts by a reluctant mother-to-be, I avoided an incubator barely and was proclaimed the "prettiest baby" in Flower Fifth Avenue Hospital by my doctor, Dr. Chilian, who may have saved my life months before when Mama had an emergency appendectomy. Or he might have been pleased with his delivery work as his timing was special. I was the first-born at 1:00 am, New Year's Day, 1928. It was a happy time before the 1929 stock market crash.

Soon I was being wheeled, in my big city carriage, by Grandpa to a nearby park where he was made a fuss over by uniformed nannies. Later after lunch, we would both nap and repeat the carriage ride in the park the next day. He was a baby expert, having raised seven of his own.

When I was five we had a big crisis. Father, one afternoon, was driving in Manhattan when he saw a crazy teenaged boy standing on a bus's back-bumper. Then he noticed it was his older son, my brother. That night, after some serious talk in German (which I did not understand) I found out Mother was in charge of our move to Long Island and the building of a house where no buses ran.

Deserting the city turned out to be not so great for Mother. While our mini-castle home (an American English Tudor) was being built, we rented a house in an unattractive section of Jamaica where the crickets kept her awake nights. I also learned not to put pussy willows in my ears for earrings. Then a lifetime experience occurred when the five year-old girl next door told me she could not play with me because I had killed Jesus. I ran in the house crying because I could not remember doing it. That night at dinner, there was a lot of talk in German which my older brother, who had had a German nanny, would not translate.

The next morning three kittens arrived, which brother and I played with on the front lawn for a week before he had to take them to find new homes. Strangely, the girl next door was in my PS 131 elementary school class for the next eight years. We never spoke in all the years.

A Teen's War

During World War II, I was a teenager with a romantic view of most things due to a lack of experience. My previous sheltered life colored my views of the world. The trials of the times caused me to become more than a bystander in spite of some early rejections.

The pride in our family grew when both brothers, hugely athletic, were shipped out to begin their military careers with the newly formed U.S. Army Ski Troops stationed at Camp Hale near Leadville, Colorado.

Father closed his meat-based business for the duration of the war to avoid twin problems. He refused either to underserve his existing clients (butcher shops and restaurants) or to get involved with black markets. He believed our military needed to feed the "Boys." I viewed Father as a great patriot.

Perhaps with all the life events during the war, one of the most memorable was Mother. She defied the federal agent who tried to recruit her to spy on the visitors to our next door neighbor, a German born professor of botany. He was a quiet man who gave me a personal tour of his dozens of different blooming azaleas, so spectacular, people would drive by when they were in bloom--a local spring ritual. Not only did Mother refuse, she let the agent know her anger.

Being too young to serve, such as in the Air Force or the hospital, I joined the American Women's Voluntary Services (AWVS) assigned to take civilian fingerprints and to staff a booth outside the movie theatre selling War Stamps.

Mother was not arrested (despite my vivid recollections) and we won the war.

"All's well that ends well!"

Think (of) It!

It's a heck (of) a thing! When I think (of) 'of' I don't know how much usage I've made (of) it. I might refer to the following, which classes sang in school daily back in my time.

> "My country 'tis (of) thee
> Sweet land (of) liberty
> (Of) thee I sing
> Land (of) the pilgrim's pride" etc. etc.

Whoever had the brainstorm to get rid (of) 'of'? Must be related to the genius who eliminated teaspoons from the table settings at your local restaurant! Never mind the extra time and efforts (of) servers. Next, they, the wise ones, will eliminate napkins. The men can make use (of) their ties instead, and women (of) their scarves - better have one!

(Of) course I recognize the needs (of) a nation at war. Didn't I help knead the yellow coloring in the butter substitute, "oleo." And many wore huaraches instead (of) leather soled shoes which required special stamps for civilian purchases. I know I did. We were proud (of) saving fat for military needs, delivering it to the butcher shop when rendered.

Frankly, I'm not in favor (of) eliminating 'of'. I think it's a heck (of) a bad idea. And I believe some (of) you love 'of' too!

"Run"

I was six or seven when three-year older brother, Mike, shouted, "Run. She has a knife!" Up the seemly endless front stairs, I flew with my two older brothers close behind.

We dashed along a hall near the servant's quarters and down the back stairs, through a door, through the garage, and down the street. With some amount of confusion, I wondered whether this was fifteen year-old Jerry's warped sense of humor or a reality. However, both brothers had followed me indoors and raced ahead outdoors to a nearby vacant lot. We stopped to rest at the fallen tree which served as our pirate ship where I gasped for air and wondered what had set her off.

Shortly I found the answer. The Principal of Jamaica High School had phoned our home and requested Jerry no longer attend there since he had stood at a classroom window and offered to help a teacher jump out as she had threatened.

Consequently, Jerry was off to Peakskill Military School with a full wardrobe and no regrets as far as I could determine. Nonetheless, his stay at the school was limited. Among other adventures, he had gone AWOL to a "house of ill repute." And for amusement, he had partly severed a leg of his dining room table so it collapsed at the next meal. The complete details of his adventures were not repeated aloud in my presence.

During the next summer at home, he received a phone call from a teacher which Mother suspected was "predatory." So in spite of having learned to stand tall, march outdoors for his various caprices, and keep a sharp crease on his trousers, Jerry concluded his formal education and became a driver at the family business.

Memories

Understandably as a teen-aged girl, I became intensely emotional as I watched my beloved Father slowly succumb to cancer. When I was younger, I enjoyed the scent of his Havana cigars and begged for their colorful paper rings.

As Father's health severely declined, Mother secured the assistance of the Red Cross to enable my ski-trooper brothers to obtain leave to visit during Father's last days. Having hidden Father's illness from my brothers, she worried the bad news might distract them from the war effort. Before traveling to Colorado, my brothers were rerouted to New York for a last goodbye. Their presence meant little to an angry teen who had, in fact, prayed for Father's release from pain and wondered where my brothers had been when Father became ill. Perhaps now, I think, being a man, Father did not want to be seen by his sons as ill, fragile, and bedridden.

Father still visits me in my memories, struggling to tell a joke as his belly shakes while his booming laughter fills the room.

R.I.P. beloved one!

Texas Thanksgiving Family Dinner

This is an unplanned first for me as I only received my flight tickets to Texas from my son a few days earlier. I am delighted to be here to help a bit in the preparations and enjoy the extended family at the ample dining room table.

The youngest participant is my great granddaughter, Mia Ross, a first born American on her father's side (he was born in Russia) and a sixth born American on her mother's side. My side of the family arrived from Germany many years ago.

Mia is truly precocious and adorable, the apple of every family member's eye, especially my son (her grandpa) who she calls "Boppa." Her smallest need is his greatest concern and it is a joy to watch them interact.

Of course, Sally, my son's wife, will take me shopping as always when I visit so I will have a beautiful outfit to wear (like putting pearls on a pig), but nevertheless a treat for me.

In my head I imagine what I will say in a few words before we dig into the banquet set before us. To God, words of appreciation that our ancestors survived through the generations and for our past and present opportunities to thrive and support each other along the way to reach the joy of this day. Tears might escape as I am recently more prone to them, but they will not be spoken of and will rapidly disappear, thank goodness.

It is possible one of my granddaughters, the unpregnant one, might offer to be the dishwasher loader, etc. Anyway, I will be excused from the job so the best dishes have a probability of longer life! I will reserve kitchen duties for my late breakfast cleanup as I will be privileged to schloff (sleep) as late as I desire. A late night of Scrabble games with my son will likely result in a 10 am rising.

Perhaps this might be my last visit, so I wish my daughter and other son and families were here as well, but greedy me cannot have the moon and stars and everything else all the time, n'est-ce pas?

More another time, perhaps!

Great Grandson, Havie, Xavier, X Man, Whatever Name You Choose

What is the key to open your locked-in self? Yes, boys can be beautiful, and you are beautiful with your dark hair and eyes that look past me at what? You love to gaze at yourself in the mirror of your great grandma's, GG's, hall closet door. Sometimes you spit at it or leave your finger prints for me to find after your visit. Now you are six years old, baby fat gone, stretching taller every time I see you.

Years ago we stood in your family's living room facing each other, I held a piece of fruit in my hand, slowing peeling it. You watched. I held a fragrant slice at you and said "tangelo" and you repeated "tangelo." Then we shared 'till it was gone. Yes, you can speak, repeat a word. Yes, GG knows you have a dictionary's worth of words locked inside your head and very slowly, word by word, your words filled with desire are slowly coming out.

Each single act of communication relieves the need for a meltdown, your tantrum-like breakdown when you are frustrated no words come through your invisible barrier. "Use your words," your parents say for your struggle is theirs, your pain and frustration are theirs as well.

To say you were a hand full to raise is an understatement. The years passed during your babyhood and toddler stages while your parents hoped you would suddenly burst out with phrases. There would be no need for consultations and a name, Autism, to rear its head and define you as someone with a barrier to normalcy.

The day came when the experts analyzed, tested, and then spoke the word. Then came the special classes, rooms with sensory aid, and teachers knowledgeable in the field of special education. Off you went on the bus to school, your parents could breathe deeply, spend time on the tasks of daily living, take courses to enhance their abilities to earn a living in a different market, catch their breaths a bit, and rejuvenate.

What pain your parents must feel listening to nieces and nephews younger in years spout their wants, needs, discoveries, and questions in a flow of paragraphs they can only pray will someday burst forth with ease from their son's lips.

In the meantime, you have traveled many places in this country and abroad with your mother's extensive family who enjoy triathlons, the wine country, and islands in pursuit of bicycle adventures, swimming, and running races with lots of togetherness and joy.

And the hugs you give leave a special glow that make us smile in your absence. And I welcomed watching you play in the hospital's water fall, forbidden joy. And if your great grandma, GG, encourages such discouraged activities it is because I can remember the intense joy of leaping into a lake, fully clothed, hands held with my forever friend, 70 years ago. Forbidden fruits truly are delectable.

I wish for a magic globe to show me your future. Until then, I rely on the wonderful stories I read about others with your condition, such as a multi-millionaire who established a fascinating, rule breaking art museum in Tasmania. Almost wordless in his childhood, he now is described as a genius as well as a gregarious adult.

With so many children being diagnosed with Autism, intensive research cannot be far behind. As I gaze into your photo, I hope all your tomorrows will wash away the memories of your early struggles with the warmth of the love all your family held for you since we touched your mother's belly before your first breath to send love then and always.

Just Do It

When your spirits sag a bit
And you find you've bit your lip.
It helps if you can take some time
To compose a nonsense rhyme.

Create a character to feature
Originate a whole new creature.
It's difficult to feel so blue
When smile or laughter overcomes you.

By Gosh, A Seusse-ical Slosh

Sunshine disappears, rain pours down
Upon orchards, farms, onto town.
Dripping white, staring, stood Dr. Seusse,
Outside his bistro, The Spruce Goose.
"My customers surely will want to sup
Soon will arrive with umbrellas up."

Munching his very last blingberry,
Suesse whooped and looked berry merry.
Soared twelve feet high in jubilation
At his fantabulous Seusse-piration!
Hopping round inside restaurant space,
Shouted he, "Transform to a watery place!"

Soon tables float just like canoes.
Patrons check hats, coats, and shoes.
Each wades to a bobbing soft seat
Where tables hold fabulous fishbowls replete
With fighting fish or galloping seahorses
Who later jump into patrons' soupy first courses.

Amazingly, diners all wear happy faces
While bouncing about in rocking places,
Or watch circling umbrellas high overhead.
While rafts deliver butterballs and warm bread,

They gape at one twenty-five foot wall,
Where flows, upside-down, a fluorescent waterfall.

Sea-breeze scented air circulates everywhere
As diners munch fabulous fresh fishy fare
Boys n' girls equally love Seusse's pride.
A whirling and swirling green water slide.
Teenagers playing wet volleyball
Bring memories parents recall.

Sighing when leaving with many a regret
Departers view the super sunny sunset
With rainbow included to make them all smile
Its colorful ark looped for at least a full mile.
A swirl and a splash at Seusse's command
Returns the Spruce Goose again to dry land.

Remember rainy days still can be fun
When Seusse-ical people do what cannot be done.

Snow, Oh No!

How southern can this capital be?
Flakes ne'er arrive to shouts of glee.
A mad rush soon ensues
Upon the dreaded snow news.
"Predicted inches soon will be
Descending on our vicinity!"

Bathroom tissue, milk and bread
In large quantities purchased ahead.
Cash registers are all ajingling
Where customers are worriedly mingling.

Before a single flake will drop,
Federal Government declares a stop.
"Leave with pay and please stay
Off the streets for the day.
We've too many traffic defeats
Besides we need to salt the streets."

Radios and TVs fuel the fear,
School closings before the storm
Questionable inches there or here
Believe me, it's the norm."

It's a rare child has a sled.
Nor do snowballs whiz by head.
Perhaps local kids think snow
Makes warts and other horrors grow.

Utilities hire temps from other states
Giving rise to future rates.
Remember still '09 power outage?
Reverberates still the outrage.

Late night til noon, blizzard rears.
Above, no airline flight soars.
The area is quite prepared.
Everyone hides, everyone's scared.

Next day, snow has disappeared.
No Armageddon as they feared.
One can scarcely find a drop,
Though silly city ground to a stop!

Snowy Morn

Tree branches robed in white
Rewarded early morn sight.
Tiny sparrows hopping by
Gave bug hunting a try.

No golf side path in view
Nor golfers playing through.
Except for birds an empty site
Did not elicit my delight.

I thought of homelessness instead
Those with neither home nor bed
While hoping deer I didn't see
Beneath some tree slept cozily.

Featherston Memories

I'm not ashamed to shed a tear.
Leisure World Writers held her dear.
She guided with gentle grace
setting Thursday's meetings pace.

Her eyes, perhaps, showed she knew
her published book she'd never view.
Yet twinkled as she knowingly spoke
about those long-gone rebel folk.

When I attended her lecture session
reviewing the War of Northern Aggression,
such research brought joy, I knew,
despite her northern Yankee view.

Under was that sense of pride
for husband's proud rebel side.
They may greet her with southern grace
when they meet in forever's place.

Unpublished, her book's without end
Yet carried inside each writer friend.
Too soon she left us grieving here.
I'm not ashamed to shed a tear.

Geessaltafreedenhaven

Gees is for the honkers who awaken me
Salt a flavor tastes just like the sea
Free, of course, is what we want to be
Den, according to the Bible where lions roar
Haven, our ancestors found on America's shore
Put them all together - geessaltafreedenhaven
Sounds German for a sneeze or shut the door
Don't throw a brick, there isn't any more.

Fragile

Angels had a pillow fight
And when I rose today
I found a feathery wonderland
Fit for penguins, ski, and sleigh.

Whitest drifts on limb and fence
Piled fluffy on the ground
Made all the world look magic
With a beauty so profound.

That I thought mischievous
Like children amongst angels
Despite their thoughtless lapses
Bring nature as they go.

If I could only stay the wind
And keep the sun asleep
This fragile kingdom could be mine
To keep, ah yes, to keep.

♦ ♦ ♦ ♦ ♦

About the Author

These are the musings of a nonagenarian. As a child, Lee treasured her library books and read (while she hid), reread, and exchanged for more books.

Lee was denied the opportunity of a four-year college education by a financially able mother, as she would only be getting married anyway. Over the years, Lee continued to pursue higher education, but did not receive her honorary diploma for lifetime achievement until bestowed by her son, a United States Attorney, in appreciation for her completing his English assignments during his years of school. She truly enjoyed the writing challenges and the several all-nighters with her son.

As a career Secretary typing 90 words per minute, Lee delighted in creating poetry. A few poems managed to survive multiple moves to be shared with her friends in the Writers Group, who inspired her to write again.

CHAPTER 2

Love Poems

By Danuta Montorfano

My Mother's Garden

She loved the Plant Kingdom
And revered Nature, as her ancestors did.
Fruit trees, bushes and flowers
Surrounded her house.

In the front garden,
Concealed by an evergreen hedge,
The fragrance of orange blossoms
Permeated the air.
Calla lilies and violas were everywhere
And a small banana tree, with its large leaves,
Made you day-dream about the tropics.

By the fence there were roses,
Red, pink and white.
Some of their branches were reaching for the beams
   of light
That filtered through the dense foliage;
Busy bees and an occasional hummingbird
Would liven up that beautiful rose garden.

In the back patio a pergola, with hanging grapes,
Led to the vegetable patch
Where carrots, horseradish and herbs intermingled,
And the tomatoes ripened under the sun.

When severe pains would strike her
She would rush, shovel in hand,
To work on her land.

Her garden gave her joy
Until the end of her life.
It was her small parcel of paradise
On the earth that she loved so much.

Edelweiss in Exile

"Oh beautiful,
Small white flower of the Alps.
So difficult to find
Even by the best mountaineers.

Far away and long, long ago,
As a small girl, I saw you
On a mountain top.
And was fascinated by your beauty.

You were like an apparition.
I touched you
And caressed your wooly and velvety hairs
With my fingertips;
A sensation I never forgot."

Then, one day, also long ago,
I saw you in a nursery
And could not resist buying you.

At home, I planted you
Outside my bedroom window,
In a small rock and moss garden.

You survived for one year
And later faded away.
I think you missed the mountains
And your sisters of the valley.

Yet your memory lives on,
Engraved in some Austrian coins
And in the imagination of dreamers.

Sleepy Town II (Blizzard of 2016)

Old man winter casts a spell.
A heavy mantle of snow covers
The whole town.
Buries cars and streets,
Sidewalks become impassable.
Winter wonderland in parks and country.
Sleepy town, sleepy town.

Breaking the all-around silence,
A few birds hopping and chirping
On the snow by the front door,
Searching for food
And flying from tree to tree.

While snowflakes keep falling
And continuing their dance macabre.
Sleepy town, sleepy town,
When will you come out of hibernation?

Lone Walker

Hot summer evening,
Dark and cloudy sky.
All is so calm…
Floating around,
By the bushes and trees,
Fireflies flashing lights.

There is no one else walking
On the sidewalks or streets.
Houses are lit,
Reminding me of Magritte's painting.
I think: Does art imitate Nature
Or Nature looks like art?

Street lights are on,
And as I head home,
Walking downhill,
Do I have a companion?
No! The long shadow ahead of me
Is my own

Afternoon in Como

Walking along the shore of the lake
With my little daughter
We stop at the candy shop
And then at a park and at a small zoo.

She is fascinated by the little chimpanzees
Bouncing and swinging from the branches of a small tree
And, napping in a corner,
A small Binturong, an exotic Asian black bear.

I treasure that small scale image
Of a little girl watching with awe
Small animals in a small zoo,
By that beautiful emerald lake
In the shadow of the Alps in Lombardy,
Very near the place
Where some of her ancestors came from.

With the beauty all around us,
And my daughter hand in hand,
This was an unforgettable trip.

The Boulevard of Yellow Flowers

Yellow dominates this week of spring.
Rows and rows of daffodils
In the gardens and the yards.
The beautiful color of these flowers
Fills my heart with joy.

In some gardens, clumps of them
Stand like bouquets, displaying their coronas.
There is an abundance of pansies
Along the curbs, themselves painted yellow.
Further up on the hills, bushes of forsythias in full bloom
Looking like walls of little fortresses.

In the sky, the clouds are outlined
By the golden glow of the setting sun.
So much yellow everywhere reminds me
Of paintings of Van Gogh
And the luminosity of Turner's landscapes.

An avalanche of memories flow through my mind:
A yellow polka dot bikini that I wore when I was young;
The yellow "cabs" of New York City;
The yellow Ferrari in the parking lot of a supermarket in
    Long Island
(Once I joked that it was mine, but one is allowed to
    dream, isn't one?)
Yellow roses and nasturtiums in my mother's garden.

Also my children's golden hair when they were little,
And the dandelion flowers they picked from the lawn
And then brought to me: "Mommy, this is for you!"

Many happy memories revived while walking
On the path along the Boulevard, this spring day,
In the midst of this glorious yellow landscape.

Separate Beds

A married couple
Shared and enjoyed
Their queen size bed
For many, many years.

Then, one day, a dark cloud
Crossed the sky and that normal,
Happy situation came to an end.
The husband, like Don Quijote,
Started to fight windmills in his dreams.
He was protecting his family, he thought.

It was all dreams,
But the fights were real.

His wife decided on separate beds.
Each one in its own.
Now, when sleep comes,
He still acts up his nightmarish dreams
But she feels safer in her bed.

Autumn Day

Gray and misty day;
Many trees are dressed in orange
And shades of yellow.
Some have shed their leaves,
That are lying like beautiful minicarpets
On the ground …

Other leaves, dry and brown, gather
On the sidewalks and curbs.
And one can see imprints of maple and oak leaves
Etched on the cement.

An occasional falling acorn breaks the silence.
A pink hue spreads in the sky, the clouds
And the horizon, as the sun sets.

I ask myself: How many more autumn sunsets
Are there left for me and my other half
Before the final sunset of our lives together?

About Postponing

Throughout the years,
I used to write or call my best friend
Quite often.
We both shared, in our background,
World War II and ancestry,
And love for the arts and volunteering.

Once, I let several months pass without calling,
Postponing …
Postponing …

And next I heard from an acquaintance
That my dear friend Dalia had died,
Still quite young.

Guilt ridden, I said to myself
No more, no more postponing.

Gifts from Nature

As I walk by a flower garden at noon,
A monarch lands on a Zinnia.
I look at its beautiful wings
And think "How amazing that it can travel
Thousands of miles in its spring migration."
I remember reading of another butterfly,
A painted lady - Vanessa cardui
That travels even farther,
Across the Sahara to Southern Europe.

In the evening, when darkness falls,
I go for another walk,
To breathe some fresh and cooler air.
I see synchronous lighting fireflies
Between the trees, at my eye level.
It is like magic, with flickering lights
On Xmas trees in summer time.

I thank Mother Nature for its generosity
In offering us these gifts
In these difficult times in our lives.

Enjoy What's Left or So Little Time

As daylight fades and stars glitter in the sky
Think of your love of family and friends.

Enjoy your dreams as you travel back in time,
Holding in your arms loves from past and present.

Embrace the time as it races by, and pray
That your prayers may be answered.

♦ ♦ ♦ ♦ ♦

About the Author

Danuta was born in Lithuania. As a young girl during World War II, she lived in Austria as a refugee. After the war, she and her family emigrated to Argentina where she resided for 17 years.

In 1962 upon graduating from medical school at the University of Buenos Aires, she married Carlos Montorfano (her lifetime soul mate) and emigrated to the United States in 1964.

Danuta and Carlos settled in Long Island, New York, where she specialized in Radiology. During her medical career, she taught residents and medical students, co-authored scientific papers published in medical journals, and she has presented scientific exhibits during radiological conferences.

Upon retiring in 2009, Danuta and Carlos moved to Leisure World of Maryland. She enjoys writing poetry about her life experiences and the camaraderie of the Writers Group.

CHAPTER 3

Poems of Love

By Carlos Montorfano

Noses, Noses

Some are big and some petite;
Some are noisy and some discreet.
Some are Roman and some are Greek
And some remind us of a beak.

Flaring nares show inner fire,
Temper, anger, love, desire.
But a wrinkle, or a twitch,
Mean foul odors ... or an itch.

People keep their noses high
If they're proud ... and low if shy.
All depends on how they feel
About their fleshy, facial keel.

But some hate the one they got
So they try to change their lot.
They expect a surgeon's knife
Will carve them a brand new life.

Some wild beasts have short cute noses
And other have a long proboscis.
Both the Elephant and the Anteater
Have theirs measured by the meter.

Envoi

Of what makes a pretty face,
The nose's deserving of first place.
I so admire a nice profile!
You could call me a "Rhino-phile"

Me!

Like a feral child of yore
I'm a creature of my whims.
And, romantic to the core,
Still beholden to my dreams.

Lest you think I'm now reformed
Let me say: "Please be reassured
I'm still stubborn as a mule
And a fool, which can't be cured."

A Red Rose?

Since the day I first saw you
I could feel a strong attraction.
But it was not love at first sight;
It was love at first olfaction.

The few times you've been away
I could not sleep, so much I missed you.
Then I thought: "I'll try to think
Of something red, to feel less blue."

At first I thought this scheme was clever,
But I'm hooked on you, forever.
It's all in vain! Your pheromones
Have overpowered my hormones.

Thanks, Mother Nature or Compensation

As we approach our middle age
Most of us will put on weight.
It won't help to starve ourselves;
To "round-out" is human's fate.

But there's no reason to feel sad
Just because our backside grows.
Life gives us that extra padding
As a cushion for her blows.

I am Full of Empty Spaces

I am full of empty spaces
Which I fill with dreams and verse.
Finding rhymes could be sheer Hell,
But some dreams can be much worse

For few things will hunt as much
As to know one dreams in vain.
So I write to make you laugh,
And that way stay half sane.

Middle Age Exercise or Why Suffer?

Some people swim
  While others strain
With all their might
  To hit a ball.
And then there're those
  For whom "SPORTS"
Consists of driving
  .... to the Mall.

To jog is fine,
  But lungs catch fire.
And, afterward,
  The knees feel sore.
So it's best to walk
  But as with sex,
If done alone
  Soon it's a bore.*

*So I've heard ...

The Descent of Man

Oh, what glorious joyful noise
Man creates with hands and voice.
Clearly, songs and music's goal
Is to calm the restless soul.

Of the classical, the best
To me is Mozart; Then the rest.
And I like both Jazz and Rock,
But my true love is Baroque.

I'm enthralled by every note
That Vivaldi ever wrote.
And who on Earth could hold a candle
To the masters, Bach and Handel?

Now I wish for, but can't find
A new sound to soothe my mind;
I will turn the dial and ZAP!
I'm attacked by rhyming crap.

Monosyllabic

To write verse is a thing I adore
(And I hope that I'll write many more)
Thought to find the right rhyme
Takes a lot of my time
And I wish that I knew what it's for.

Memory

The tree of life has grown another ring
Around its inner core
But, being a tree, won't remember a thing
Of all the rings it's grown before.

Like trees, we will grow old
And our memories will fade away.
But, before we turn forever cold,
There is this I want to say:
Whereas I can't (or won't) forget,
What I hope is you might recall
That fateful day when we last meet,
If you remember me at all.

My Music

I must confess that, quite often,
I've felt more than a little sad.
But I'm not scared of the future,
Nor I get stuck in the past.

At least, in rhyme, I tried,
Though late, to open my soul.
And though there're goals I'll never reach
I accept my Destiny in peace.

Because, sooner or later, I'll be
One more note in the vast space.
To, at the end, fade away,
As the shadow of what I once was.

Nobody is Perfect or The Secret of Life

Even doctors can catch colds,
And attorneys can get sued.
The best trackers can get lost
And psychiatrists, unglued.

Tennis pros with the best serve
At times fail and hit the net.
An umpire may miss a call:
No one's hit a thousand, yet.

There's no perfect human being,
For even sailors can get sick.
So love a lot and learn to laugh,
And enjoy what makes you tick.

I am Obvious

Like they say of circus' clowns
I've been known to shed a tear
I could never hide the truth,
For my eyes make me sincere.

As you look at me you'll know
If I'm happy or in despair.
You can see right through my soul;
I'm transparent like clean air.

Music to My Ears

Though I'd never be accused
Of having said something profound
Words keep pouring out of me
For I love the way they sound.

Woolgathering

By now, I know I won't be rich,
But found that writing is my niche.

At times my syntax needs repair,
But writing verses beats despair.

And I would spend a lot of time,
Fighting anguish with my rhyme.

So seldom now I think of death.
I'll save that chore for my last breath.

◆ ◆ ◆ ◆ ◆

About the Author

Carlos (1936-2018), a retired medical doctor, married his lifetime soul mate, Danuta. His light verse and prose was inspired by (among others) the limerick obituary of an ornithologist, the humorist writings of Ogden Nash, and professor of English Richard Armour.

    Carlos enjoyed writing light verse, limericks (clean ones), and haiku. A few of his better verses were published in local newspapers in Latin America and the United States.

CHAPTER 4

What's It All About

By Gladys Blank

Remembering the Good Times

I had two rather disturbing phone calls yesterday morning. Disturbing may not be the best way to explain it, but definitely calls that left me thinking for some time about why are we here, how long will we be here, and what can we do to help not only ourselves but those we care about to cope with life's trials and tribulations.

The first call came about 7:10 am! Needless to say, I immediately assumed it was someone to relay some definitely "disturbing" news, a lost job, a break-up of some kind, an illness, or (even worse) the death of someone I care about. I answered the phone immediately, of course, prepared for who knows what. The caller was Carol, the daughter of my significant other who passed away two years ago. She calls occasionally, to sort of keep in touch with me, often in subtle ways, thanking me for being there for her Dad in his last year or two when illnesses of one type or another became constant reminders of his declining health.

This call though was somewhat different. She was apparently feeling melancholy, unhappy, perhaps lonely, and just needed to connect with someone who was not necessarily a family member, but someone who could appreciate and empathize with how she was attempting to cope with what the future will hold for her, even if not putting it exactly in those words.

And so, trying to sound cheerful as possible, I asked all the right questions about her siblings, their comings and goings, the happy events in her life and theirs, commenting enthusiastically about this happening, that event. The call ended on a better note than it had started and we promised each other we would get together soon.

The second call was from Bill, my close friend's son to inform me his Mother was in the hospital with serious cardiac problems. That was another disturbing call, fraught with worry and anxiety about what comes next inasmuch as my friend is 90 years young. Did I want to go with him to visit her for a short time? Of course, I could not say no, and so the rest of the day had me in not the best frame of mind.

In the end, I finally realized the best way to cope with life's less than happy times is to remember the GOOD TIMES in one's life. Being married to a career serviceman (Coast Guard) and stationed in Hawaii for five years was truly a time to be treasured as was our 54 years of marriage. Meeting a man while I was already a senior, who was to become my significant other for seven wondrous years was another memorable time. And needless to say, being the proud mother of two successful children and the grandmother of a granddaughter climbing the ladder of success as a chemical engineer at Merck Chemical company and a grandson making his mark in the I-Tech world are all a big part of the GOOD TIMES.

What's next for me? Going to call Eyre Bus and Tours and sign up for a trip on a fall foliage tour on the Skyline Drive with a visit to an art gallery and lunch in Luray.

At Sea

For many years my family (son and his wife, daughter and her husband) have been suggesting or mentioning and finally subtly (a true oxymoron) urging me to plan some kind of get away in which we can be together, because no one knows given my advanced age (my choice of words) how many opportunities there may be to do just that - to spend a happy time together.

And so, on one of my better days, meaning feeling physically and emotionally on a slightly higher plain than is often the case, I began a random surfing excursion on the Internet. Given my unwritten dossier includes my 20 year stint as a Travel Agent, it wasn't so difficult a task.

I started by perusing various cruise lines, since over the years I had accumulated a variety of so-called points or rewards on some of the cruise lines sailing from the East Coast. And there it was! The Princess Cruise Line was having a sale, as they put it. For a rather reasonable rate they were offering what I thought was at least worth considering - a short 5N/6D cruise out of Fort Lauderdale to a couple of stops in the Caribbean that I had not previously visited. The more I checked into the ins and out, when and hows, the more I came to believe this might be just what my kids and their kids might approve and enjoy. Needless to say, they were totally on board.

And so having travel agent experience, I booked the flights to Fort Lauderdale for one and all and the staterooms with the help of my PC and the cruise person with whom I chatted on line.

Now comes the feeling of being "At Sea" and becoming somewhat anxious and apprehensive about this adventure as the date for taking off looms just a week away. Though I talk daily with my daughter as she sits at her desk in her office most mornings awaiting the arrival of fellow employees, and I have meaningful conversations many Sunday mornings with my son in Allentown, Pennsylvania. I do not spend very much time with either one of them.

As a result, they are not really aware of my limited ability to dash about from one activity to another, on this tour, on that tour, a walking trip, exercise routine, exploring on foot the terrain of this island and that island, etc. etc. Rather, I am simply looking forward to good food served in pleasant surroundings, a walk or two, though labored, to the casino and the evening entertainment, a little sauntering through the various shops, having my cabin taken care of, the hope of great weather in the Caribbean and, of course, just the companionship of being with them.

Having always been the very active, involved, energetic individual they have known all their lives, how will they see, understand, and accept the passage of years and the inevitable changes that have taken place in my life.

Trying to see the cup half full (as my daughter constantly lectures me to do), it's time to start packing. I have already gotten a friend to do a short shopping trip with me in search of a great handbag, just prefect for being At Sea.

Ides of March

What does the Ides of March mean? It's not about the assassination of Julius Caesar. Have you ever been greeted by someone on the infamous day by saying "beware the Ides of March?" that sure doesn't sound very joyous, so what are the Ides of March and should you really be worried about them?

The Latin root of "ides' means "to divide," so the word basically just denotes the middle of the month. The Roman calendar designates the 15th as the Ides of March, May, July, and October. But the calendar is not what made the Ides of March famous. This was the assassination of

Julius Caesar on March 15 in 44 BC. One if the most famous murder plots organized by Marcus Brutus, a young protégé of Caesar's, as a way to put an end to the power-hungry "Dictator for Life." Since then the Ides of March has come to be known as an unlucky day. But is it really such as bad day? Apparently a host of other bad things have happened on the day throughout history including a cyclone hitting Samoa in 1889, the German occupation of Czechoslovakia in 1939, and the cancellation of the Ed Sullivan Show in 1971 according to the Smithsonian. Beware the Ides of March indeed.

Before Caesar's assassination, the word "ides" was just a calendar term to mark the full month, but after his death the day took on its new portentous meaning, a day when prophesies of doom are realized. A look at the Washington Post's homepage could support the theory that bad things happen on the Ides of March. The Taliban suspended peace talks with the United States, the Republican Party is becoming a full-out brawl, the situation in Syria is only getting worst, and HBO cancelled the racetrack drama "Luck" after a third horse died on the set.

But bad things happen every day, we just notice them on days of heightened superstition like the Ides of March and Friday the 13th.

What does all of the aforementioned have to do with me? I had a particularly restless night one day this week, unable to fall asleep and exhausted from twisting and turning in an attempt to find the right place to be. I finally gave up, sat up, and the whole concept of the ides came to mind as I sat there remembering what a rough month March had been for me starting with a serious long lasting viral respiratory infliction that would not say goodbye, the 5-night Caribbean cruise to Dominican Republic and Grant Turk Island I had arranged for my family was not nearly as exciting as I had thought it might be, and the long tiring ride to Allentown to celebrate Passover only to be followed by a recurrence of that cold I had hoped was long long gone, news of another shooting, the unseasonable cool cool weather and I didn't even get to see "The Shape of Water."

Nevertheless, March is now gone and I am looking forward to April, cherry blossoms and a long anticipated concert featuring Keith Lockhart and the Boston Pops at Strathmore Sunday afternoon.

Book Club

I am a member of a book club that meets once a month to discuss the book assignment of the month and to socialize with members of the club over light refreshments. I am an avid reader but normally prefer to read certain genres--novels dealing with older folk and their various trials and tribulations. Needless to say, I usually relate to their problem, that problem, or a pleasant event of last week, or years ago, experienced by someone much like me. From time to time, a good memoir or non-fiction account of "what's happening out there" will attract my attention as well.

I joined the club in the hope I would get to know others who shared my love of books and my special interests. However, the club has turned out to be something entirely different than expected. Various members of the club have suggested books that I would never take off the shelf. In any case as a loyal member, I give each suggested book a read. But truthfully, I've not been particularity overwhelmed by their suggestions.

When my turn came to suggest a book, I immediately selected J.D. Vance's "Hillbilly Elegy." If you have the time, please put it on your bucket list. To quote from two of the many recommendations on the book jacket, "You will not read a more important book about America this year," and "Never before have I read a memoir so powerful and so necessary."

But back to me, having been born, raised, and lived as more or less a member of what I would call the upper middle class, I never gave much thought as to how many other Americans less fortunate lived, worked, and died in our country. The story of "Hillbilly Elegy" was a shocking revelation for me, with the political climate being what it is, with talks of populism, nativism, the struggles of the lower middle class, economic inequality, etc. Mr. Vance's memoir says it all. He grew up in a rural area of Kentucky, where most of those employed worked in the coal mines, few children got an education as far as high school. Most families lived from small paycheck to the next small paycheck. Many men, bemoaning their situation in life, spent a lot of time with their buddies in the local pub. Very few people in Appalachia country felt their situation in life mattered to the rest of us, or that their lives could ever change for the better.

Needless to say, Mr. Vance, who was brought up in a large although loving dysfunctional family unit, had no greater goals than any of his friends. He was devoted to his grandmother and his grandfather who wanted more for their favorite grandchild. They always encouraged him to do better to escape the confines of their poor surroundings. The story is an intriguing and eye-opening saga of what can be accomplished with encouragement and determination.

At one point in the book, Mr. Vance described his four years in the United States Marine Corps. He wrote the Marines assumed maximum ignorance from the enlisted folks. They assumed no one has taught you anything about physical fitness, personal hygiene, or personal finances. He took mandatory classes about balancing a checkbook, savings, and investing. In fact, he spoke extremely highly of the positive influence the Marine Corps had on his life.

The Marine Corps was the first to give him an opportunity to truly fail. They made him accept any challenge and then when he did fail, gave him another chance. In the Marines, he went on to say, he saw men and women of different social classes and races work as a team and bond like family.

Mr. Vance, encouraged by his grandmother, enrolled in Ohio State University even though he did poorly in high school. He graduated from college while working three jobs to meet his financial obligations, then achieves a successful career as a lawyer.

The life lesson of the book is to demonstrate how many Americans are merely existing in this country of so-called opportunity but given the proper encouragement and assistance can have a better life.

♦ ♦ ♦ ♦ ♦

About the Author

Gladys is a native Philadelphian. During her professional life, she has traveled the world as a busy Travel Agent married to a career Coast Guard serviceman. Her career also included service as an office manager at a large middle school in Philadelphia. She moved to Maryland after retirement to be closer to family and grandchildren.

At Leisure World, Gladys is active in many clubs and activities. She serves as the Co-President of Na'Amat, an organization that raises funds for needy women and children in Israel. She is an avid bridge player and enjoys the game of Mah Jong. She volunteers for the Rossmoor Library, signs up for interesting classes, and always looks forward to participating in the Writers Group.

CHAPTER 5

Life

By Grace Cooper

Big Little Things

Not diamonds,
Not pearls,
Not huge bank accounts,
No need for these

So welcome,
A smile
A touch,
A call on the phone,
The sound of a voice,

Not the world's riches,
As time moves on,
Most cherished are
Human connections
As we reach the end

Four

One
White
All are good people

Two
Red
Guns and such

Three
Black
Sitting on the street
Hungry in the Tents

Four
Pale
All gone

T'is Of Thee

Across the Mall
Saltine crumbs float
Forgotten pillars of vanquished monuments
Once tall columns blow
In powdered flakes
Clowns parade pathetically
Trying to glue symbols together
Grotesque smiles covering flimsy non documents
Heroes weep
Children scream!
Crumbs drift away in darkness ...

Night

Love crosses darkness
Gently lies beside
Under covers
Never alone

The Day After Tomorrow

Unlost figures
Linger on cave walls,
Earthen jars
Spill out fragile scrolls,
Crumbling words
On disappearing papers
Pencils, quills, pens,
Break into dust,
New words
Preserved?
In the Cloud
Click "print"
The Sun laughs

Misty

Dreams of veiled dress
White satin shoes
Loving caresses
Sweet words of caring
Scattered
Pasted together
Falling apart
Leaving

Refitting
Again
Knives
And roses
Lost beginning
Fake restarts
Bullets and promises
Look ahead
Move on
Ever shrinking horizon
Fade to black

Three A. M.

Reach for a hand
Find a pillow instead
Toss
Turn
Hug the pillow
Toss it on the floor
Fingers grip the sheets
Doze
Pull up the blanket
Turn
Darling
Sweetheart
Turn
A pillow
Move over
Where?
Reach for a hand that isn't there.

Knit One

Sunshine sparkles
Happy children
Run and jump with smiling faces
Purl two
Rain drops patter on the window
Keeping pace with quiet memories
Knit one
Swiftly moves the moon's phases
Purl two
Chalk boards
School books
Plaids and tweeds
Knit one
Pretty dresses
Bow to society
Purl two
Shattered dreams
Patched with tomorrows
Knit one
Help twisted with misunderstandings
Hot sunshine
Thunder showers
Hidden dreams
Hopeless loves
Purl two
Grey with wrinkles
Blue surroundings
Knit one
Purl two

Night Shadows

Every tomorrow never comes,
Every dream is etched on pillows
Every wish is wrapped in hopes
All the words are someone else's
Turn toward stardust
Eyes closed yet more opened
Felt caresses floating on air of midnight
Remembered day echoes
Remembered words
Lying on clouds
Acting as soft touch

Winter Love

Drinking hot cocoa
Wrapped in cozy robes
Watching shows together
Away from howling winds
Legs wrapped lightly around each other
Soft kisses "goodnight"
Soft music
Soft caresses
Away from outside's soft snow
Close and snuggly
"Yes, I love you
Just move over a little
And change the channel
Before you turn out the light."

Facade

Hot steamy shower
Spray of cologne
Silky lingerie
Colorful dress
Bright sunny smile
Cheerful hello
Witty conversation
Sparkly goodbye
Breakable

♦ ♦ ♦ ♦ ♦

About the Author

Grace was born in Washington, DC and lived there during the years of enforced segregation. She learned to read at the age of two and started her writing career at the age of five when one of her poems appeared in her elementary school newspaper. She also wrote and drew cartoon strips for her young friends.

Grace married after graduation from Dunbar High School, the first high school in Washington DC - not just the first high school for the "colored" children as some think. She continued her education, first working and going to school part time, later receiving scholarships for college study as she raised a family of four children. She received the Bachelor of Science in Secondary English Education from DC Teachers College, the Master of Science in Urban Language from Federal City College, and Doctor of Philosophy in Psycholinguistics from Howard University. She took additional graduate work at Georgetown University and received a special faculty grant for study in Biblical studies at Yale University.

LIFE

Throughout her life, her writing continues. Much of her work life focused on her writing skills. She published many articles and books during her career including: public relations for the C & P Telephone Company, language research for George Washington University, writer for The Child Welfare League of America, and several teaching positions in English, history, and art, from junior high school through university level.

Twice she received special faculty grants for summer work at the United States Central Intelligence Agency.

After retiring, she continued writing and was a poet for the Takoma Park Senior Citizens program, which featured many of her poems in its newsletter, and presented regular poetry readings for the public. She left the position once she moved to Leisure World in Montgomery County.

Grace was also co-founder of the M Ensemble Company of Miami Florida, for which she wrote articles for The Miami Herald and plays for the company. Upon her return to Washington DC, she wrote and had produced several plays, many for the Howard University Players. Her most widely produced play was a children's play, written for the debut of the Howard University Children's Theater, "Kojo and the Leopard." The play has been performed by schools, universities, and other groups around the country and was reviewed in The Washington Star. She has written novels, short stories, and poetry. Writing poetry is her current love.

CHAPTER 6

A Few Captured Thoughts

By Radha Pillai

A Wishful Thinking

Order is born out of chaos
The 'big bang' created the world
Color mixes made master-pieces
Beautiful melodies often come from agonies
Agitation makes clothes come clean
Babies come from a lot of commotion
Harsh winter brings out colorful spring

Our world is in a lot of chaos now
What beauty or perfection could we or should we
Expect to come out of all that?

Big Old Banyan Tree

They say it is thousands of years old, no one knows for sure. The stories people heard about the tree are always the same; it was there for as long as they can remember. No one remembers any story about when the little sapling started. All stories depict the big tree with its magnificent canopy which extended several meters around. It was home to several types of birds, squirrels, monkeys and god only knows what other animals and insects it homed.

There is a large square cement platform around the base of the tree with several burrows going into its base from different directions, which proves the base is home for another set of life including rodents, lizards, families of ants, and maybe a few snakes. The cement square is also the village center, all the major business and social activities of the village take place there from morning till late at night. There is more than one barber cutting hair or shaving a face; there are tailors stitching outfits; soothsayers and palm-readers; letter-writers and document preparers; paan sellers and tea stalls with spicy fritters and nuts; old women selling banana-leaf packets of breakfast, lunch or dinner depending on the time of the day.

The entire village comes to the tree at least once a day; young and old alike, if they can move they come on their own, and if they cannot someone will move them there. There are not many rich people in the village. Whether you are rich or poor they are all equal under the tree. They all look happy to be part of the group. If you are an outsider from a faraway place it doesn't matter, you are treated equally. At least it seems that way, unless you do not understand the language. Even then, if you have an interpreter, you can mingle in easily.

On any particular day you might be able to see a wedding, a funeral, or a baby's birth announcement. Everyone celebrates or moans together. If it rains or pours, umbrellas will open up everywhere; some even put up little tents. If it gets a little chilly, people will start little fires here and there with pieces of twigs collected from somewhere and anyone can gather around and continue the conversations.

When night falls little oil or kerosene lamps come to life under the tree. Activities continue without any break. When they get tired, they leave one by one to sleep, to refresh, and come back in the morning to continue what they left behind. A few with no place to go will linger on and find their cozy corners, open their mats, curl up, and pull some rags to cover themselves, and sleep until the village roosters trumpet arrival of daylight.

I assume the big old tree must have acquired a lot of knowledge from all those people from all those years of activities under its elaborate canopy. I hope the old tree can live forever and the (seemingly) peaceful life that goes on under the tree is true and continues to be true forever.

Earth's Lament

Deforestation just pulled off my blanket
Strip-mining later skinned me alive
Looking for oil they went even deeper
Fracking for gas even deeper and wider

Corporate farming and landscaping experts
Covered me with chemicals and GMO seeds
"Produce", they demanded, "the right way - our way"
Forced labor is something that I cannot live with

Smoke spewing chimneys, CO_2 emissions
Plastics all over which I cannot digest
Hormones and drugs in food chains and landfills
Too much to chew, I'm dying of sickness

I'm trying to fight back with thunder and lightning
Continuous pounding with rain, sleet and snow
Ground get so swollen it ends in expulsion
Drowning the land and pulling those mud slides

Twisters that churn all through their paths
Wild fires, sink-holes, strong wide and deeper
More bugs, more pollen, more sickness, more death
High-tides, tsunami, floods, droughts and quakes

Changes in seasons with long lasting winters
Spring and fall shortened, summers extended
A war I am fighting, trying to stay on
So, 'Help Me' before it's too late

"Progress" they say "Don't you want progress?"
Progress is good, but, please, do it with sense
For goodness sakes children, don't make a mess
"Crying wolf" they say "Mother Earth is tougher"

You don't make sense, think for a moment
One last reminder, take as a warning
I'm committing suicide, you know what that means
You will be gone before I will be done

Ethics, Morality, Civics, etc...

Where are we in the big picture? Can you spot us?
Does it matter anymore?
Teachers are pressured to teach for test scores
They don't have the luxury to focus on character or ethics
Parents don't have the time or patience, let alone the
  know-how

To teach their children ethics, morality or civic duties
Our leaders are not in a position to stand as role-models for their citizenry
Does it matter anymore?
Survival of the fittest! We have gone back!
Regressed to the animals we originated from!
All the development, research, applications and progressions!
Does it matter anymore?
Would you turn in your friend if you believe he or she committed a crime that harmed several people?
If it is your son or daughter, husband or wife, mother or father, would you?
Does it matter anymore?
Does a crime committed by a member of your religion is of lesser consequence to you than a similar crime committed by a member of another religion?
Does it matter anymore?
Does honesty, inclusiveness, empathy and moral courage mean anything to you?
Is cheating OK if it results in winning or being successful?
Is bullying OK? Is physical or verbal stereotyping OK?
Does it matter anymore?
It seems narcissism is on the rise in this world
Whose responsibility is it to speak against the systemic injustices and racism in this world?
Does it matter anymore?
Finally, whose job is it to put an end to the corrosive, divisive national politics?
Does it matter anymore?

If

If I have the power to be,
Whatever I want to be
What would I like to be?
The sound that fills the world?
The love that fills the mind?
The sun that brings the life?
The earth that bears that weight?
The hand that heals the hurts?
The rains that cleanse the dirt?
The light that clears the dark?
The wind that lulls the nature?
The food that soothes the palate?
The drink that quenches the thirst?
The flower with sweet fragrance?
The power of pen? The color of rainbow?
Oh! What else, what else would I like to be?
For now, I am quite happy in my hides
Without my supernatural powers

Live the Moment

Sweet memories, sometimes bitter sweet
Sad memories, sometimes terribly sad
Funny memories, sometimes hilariously funny
Bitter memories, sometimes unbearably bitter
Memories are "past"- moments that came and gone
Do we have any control over the "past"?
Past is past and that is that!!!
We are making our past from future

Future comes in one fluttering, tempting moments at a time
We have the power to shape it, mold it, caress it, and savor it before it goes
We have no power to hold it, stop it, possess it, reject it or prolong it
The moment it leaves us it joins forces with the past
And becomes part of our memories
Therefore, we have all the power in the world to make
Memories the way we want it to be
Ready, get set, go
You have no time to prepare
Make all the moments count
Make them all sweet and memorable

Nothing at All

What is heaven like? Do we know?
We expect it to be peaceful, yes tranquil for the mind
Will we have a mind when we get there?
Pleasant weather, auto-adjusted for everyone
Sun shining just right, few cumulous clouds
Pleasing for the eyes. Will we have eyes?
Green rolling hills, beautiful flowers, colorful butterflies
Tall trees, winding rivers, gentle breeze
Lakes, oceans, mountains, valleys
Animals big and small, all tame and pettable
Foods pleasing for every palate, will we have palates?
Delicious, no concern for calories
Drinks, soothing, thirst quenching, intoxicating
Music that stimulates individual tastes

Will we have eyes, ears, hands and mouths when we get there?
But then, what do we want to look like?
Little butterflies, humans with wings?
How about plumes of steam, a whiff of air? Maybe, just nothing at all
We don't want to stay at one place, do we?
We would like to be in places where we wish to be, instantly
So the "Nothing at all" makes more sense
We need company. Don't we? We could all be together
A group of - bunch of - pool of - ocean of
No - a world of "Nothing at all"

Spring

Finally, spring has arrived. Hurray! Hurray!
After that bitter cold pipe-bursting winter
With hail storms, ice storms and blanketing snow
Road closings, school closings, pile-ups and traffic jams
Slipping, sliding and salt-spreading trucks
Spring has arrived. Hurray! Hurray!
Blue jays that screeches, finches and doves
Sparrows, cardinals, starlets in troves
Robins, chickadees and so many more
Spring has arrived. Hurray! Hurray!
Forsythias pulling their bright golden veils
Crocuses peeking, snowdrops are popping
Beauty cups, butter cups, daffodils and tulips
Bushes and trees bulging with buds
Eager to show their beauty in blooms

Honeybees are buzzing looking for food
Spring is here. Hurray! Hurray!
Rabbits are hopping, the deer herds are grazing
Grass blades are greening, pollen keep floating
Itching and sneezing and noses are dripping
Spring is here. Hurray! Hurray!

Nuggets from My Memory Chest

My great grandma's house was in the country - an old traditional house in the middle of a cluster of great big farms. To my young mind it felt like you walked for miles and miles through mango groves, paddy fields, tapioca farms, banana plantations, rows and rows of coconut trees, cattle grazing fields, chicken coops, and vegetable gardens to get to it. Great grandma grew practically everything they needed; anything left over they traded for the remaining needs. No refrigeration, no electricity, and no telephone.

We, the city dwellers got a big kick out of visiting grandma's house every summer; and we looked forward to it every year. Even better was when we went to great grandma's house a few miles away. For that trip we got up early in the morning, ate a big breakfast, and started the walk before the sun got hot. The path was narrow. The best part of the trip was through the mango groves and the tapioca farms. We liked to climb the mango trees, especially when it was close to harvest time. The best mangoes were the ones who had just gotten ripe on the tree, just right before the birds or the squirrels got to it. Just bite into it, eat the fleshy part and throw the rest away and keep repeating until you get sick of it.

The tapioca is an entirely different experience. Tapioca is usually planted on rows of foot-high mounts of dirt to facilitate easy harvesting. The planting is done by cutting the tapioca stem into foot-long pieces and sticking them on top - three per mount diagonally - half in the mount and the other half sticking out. About three to seven long roots grow down each of these stems and slowly grow thicker. We loved to dig out the young root when it gets to be a little thicker than a carrot. Shell out the skin and it is sweet and crispy. If you eat too much you could get sick because it has a toxin that affects your brain. That is why when you cook tapioca, you boil the pieces in water and drain it first.

By the time we reach great grandma's house we usually are pretty full. There was no way to warn great grandma of our visit. She only knew we would show up one of the days in summer. After our arrival she would start preparing for our meal. She would ask us to collect our favorite vegetables from her garden. She had string beans, snap peas, snake goads, bitter goads, cucumbers, squashes, okra, eggplant, purple and green leafy vegetables, sweet potatoes, and many more types of vegetables. Then you had to help with the shelling, cutting, or peeling. We would eat some of it while helping. Then we leave everything and walk down to a stream that flows through her property. We jump into it, swim and take a bath. Tired and hungry by the activities we return to the enticing fragrance of great grandma's kitchen. The way she cooked with the spices and coconut (that the maid ground on the stone) was really delicious. You eat and eat until you are overfull.

The nights were filled with exchanges of stories, games, and songs from both young and old. The noise level will go higher and higher for a while and then slowly one by one will get quiet and all will fall asleep, sometime by early morning. Sleeping late though is not possible in such households because the roosters, the cows, and birds of all tunes will be making a big racket before the sun is up. The breakfast smell from the kitchen is too hard to resist even when your body says to sleep. So you get up, eat breakfast, and start the trip back to grandma's house, unless we decide to stay for another day or two.

Those were the days!!!

The Human Ingenuity

Eagles roaming round and round
Must be something on the ground
Acute vision from above
Wouldn't you like that? Who wouldn't?

World is full of similar wonders
Bees can retrace hundreds of miles
Butterflies travel thousands of miles
Dogs can follow infinite smells
Fish can decode intricate voice
Birds can remember time and space
Snakes can sense the slightest of shakes
Littlest of seeds grow to thousands of feet
How do animals eat one thing and not the other?

We have ways to figure these out
And to create wonders anew
By stretching limits our brain provides
Appreciate and thank the ingenuity
We, the humans have to offer

The Sacred River

I was there at The River
They told me I could get relief from my sins
I took great troubles to get to it,
Spent resources I couldn't afford; spent time I couldn't spare
I was there at The River
They told me this River started in heaven
Some sage brought it down to earth

With austerities and penances performed for the cause
So that the land and the people could get relief
I was there at The River

They told me I should submerge my body in its waters
Say a prayer or two listing my sins and requests
Offer some money and flowers to the pundits nearby
He, of course not she, has direct connections to God it seems
I was there at The River

It so happened the day I got there
I saw writing about The River on the local paper
The bacteria count was thousands of times the accepted limit
I was there at The River

Should I submerge myself in these sacred waters?
Thousands, not hundreds do it every year
To shed their sins and reserve a place in heaven
I was there at the River

I saw the calm and peace on the faces of the pilgrims
Wet, fully clothed coming off the River
They believe their souls are clean and death can only lead
  them to heaven

The River, rushing, gushing with no worries in the world
Carrying all the sins and pollution dropped by the millions
I was there at The River

Should I shed my sins and get a coating of the germs?
Hmm... What sins do I have to shed?
I sat and thought about it for a while
Evaluated my life, a few minutes of soul searching
I decided my sins are not really sins and didn't need shedding
I was there at The River

But, just in case
I imagined myself immersed in that polluted,

Sin-burdened water
Prayed, listed my sins and requests
Paid the pundit at the shore and returned to my hotel
I was there at The River
I felt relieved somehow
Maybe because I thought about my past
Maybe because I thought about my sins
Maybe because I thought about my future
Maybe because I made my requests in my prayers
I felt relieved of all my burdens in life
I was there at The River

You Are What You Eat

Grandma's old recipe - good old wheat, stone-ground
Did she use yeast packets or
Did she harvest from the surroundings?
Cranberries, blue berries, nuts of all kinds
Pumpkins, squash, seasonal veggies
How did she make it? Delicious and nutritious
You are what you eat my friend, you are what you eat

Partially, no, fully hydrogenated
Gluten free, GMO, milled and bleached
Added ground bark for fiber, micro-beads for texture
Natural flavors that come out of labs
Mmm ... it is so soft and fragrant, you just can't resist
You are what you eat my friend, you are what you eat

Germicide, pesticide, glyphosate and the like
No worms or fungi can survive in your fruits and veggies
Neither the helpful gut microbes if you eat them

Don't worry; you get more than what you asked for
Through run off to your drinking water supply
You are what you eat my friend, you are what you eat

Chemical companies make money, awful lot of your money
They don't care about anyone's health;
They care only about their bottom line
They'll use any old crooked ways to brain-wash you and
  your children
The scientists get paid for finding good flavors
For finding good tastes and finding good textures
The developers get paid for making good products
The marketers get paid for selling more products
The companies get rewarded if stock prices jump
CEOs get rewarded by bonuses and perks
Unless you resist with you valets, their valet wins
You are what you eat my friend, you are what you eat

Chemical baths to prevent untimely sprouting of potatoes
  and onions
Wilting or rotting spinach and kale
Fungicide laced waxes on fruits and veggies
To look their best and keep the fruit-flies away
Package it in BP-A laden plastics or Styrofoam
My grandma would be thrilled if she could see these
Perfectly formed greens and fruits with no speckles or spots
Might even think they are made out of wax
And keep them as show-pieces next to her vase
You are what you eat my friend, you are what you eat

Cooked, processed, packaged and ready to eat
Microwave in plastic or boil the pouch in water
Or, just open the can heat it and eat
Wonderful time savers, delicious in no time
Don't check ingredients, your grandma will choke?
You are what you eat my friend, you are what you eat

My grandma never heard of ADHD or COPD
ED or UTI or any of these modern acronyms
That we are so familiar with and take thousands of pills
 to treat
Spare her; may her soul rest in peace
You are what you eat my friend, you are what you eat

Fate

Do you believe in Fate? I always wonder!

I have heard people say, "The Indians are fatalistic. They believe the future happens according to a pre-destined fate. What you do or do not do is pre-planned for you." However, the Hindu epics emphasize over and over, "Do your best or what you think is best without being overly concerned about the end result. That is your duty in life."

The acceptance of a pre-destined fate supported the basis of the caste system. Ego, pride, and prestige were defined by benign task-based categories and became your fate. The highest caste were the group who ministered to the symbols of God as they claimed they are the only ones who could talk to God. The group who protected them and ruled the land became the next highest caste. The traders and suppliers of goods became the third in ranks; and the service sector became the fourth. Whoever was opposed to categorization became "the untouchables or the caste-less." Even within the caste there are several sub-castes and sub-sub categories with higher and lower rankings. Only the elders in the community can really tell the exact markings. The markings become clear mainly when it comes to marriages. Such and such family is below our caste and therefore their children should not get married to our children. Your birth (or your fate) decides your caste. In recent times, a person's education and mobility is taking baby steps in erasing the deep cut markings of caste distinctions in Indian society. Maybe in a couple of hundred years the caste system will be a thing of the past. But then, what other system will replace it is yet to be understood.

I always wonder with great perplexity how I ended up where I am. While growing up, I never thought of moving out of India and living somewhere on a permanent basis. It just happened.

My husband and I were teaching college in a not-so-crowded city of South India in the early 1960s. Several American Peace Corps members approached with a request to teach them the local language. The lessons started in earnest twice a week at our house. They would usually bring their newsletters, newspapers, and magazines from home in the United States and every so often would leave them for us after they were done with them. In one newsletter, we found a small two-line ad for teachers in a college in Hollywood, Florida. We found out later, the college was a front for draft-dodgers of the Vietnam era. No matter, we got to Miami and were received with great pomp and fan-fare. The Miami Herald published our photographs and details in an article covering almost half a page, the beginning of our struggles-to-come, and the shaping of the bright future to follow.

A two-line ad in a discarded newsletter - was that my destiny, my fate?

Do I really believe in fate? I always wonder!

Each person I meet, each situation I come across, each opportunity I missed, each opportunity I gained - were they pre-destined for me?

Rock Creek Trail

Wooded trails, gentle breeze
Rattling leaves, chirping birds
Rays of sunlight through the trees
Flowing water, gurgling waves
Turtles lined up on fallen twigs
Sunning themselves like birds on cables
Occasional herons still as statues
Waiting for the fish to swim by
Trees are in their glorious colors
Orange, red, green, and yellow
Some are even turning brown
Pretty soon they shed them all
And wait for winter to come and go
Winding trails by the creek
Over and under bridges and roads
By the lake, by the creek, by the park, by the field
Kids play football, soccer, tennis
Cyclists zoom by shouting, "On your left, on your left, thank you"
Novice hikers freeze in middle
Are they coming on the left or do they want you on the left
But they always find a way and pass you waving.

♦ ♦ ♦ ♦ ♦

About the Author

Radha was born in south India and emigrated to the United States in the mid 1960's. Her diverse professional career includes: a science teacher in public schools in North Carolina and New York; a research assistant for a New York patent law firm; and a chemist for a photographic film company. Upon obtaining an MBA from the New York Institute of Technology, Radha worked in the mortgage banking industry. She has over 10 years of volunteer service including 3 years for the Volunteers in Service to America (VISTA). She relocated to Leisure World in 2006 and joined the Writers Group of Leisure World in 2007.

CHAPTER 7

World Traveler

By Jane Hawes

A Bushy Tale

When I was young I remember lying in bed and hearing a scratching and peeping noise up in the attic above my room. My parents also heard it so an exterminator was called in and discovered a squirrel nest, mother and babies. He took them away. A few days later, I heard more scratching. I had to convince my father to go to the attic to see what it was. At first, he saw nothing and then as he was about to leave he saw something small barely moving. It was a baby squirrel that the exterminator had overlooked. He brought it downstairs. Mom and I thought it was so cute and almost dead so we called the nature center to see what to do.

They said they had a squirrel cage and to put the baby on a heating blanket inside. We were to feed it milk with an eye dropper and it might recover. We followed the instructions as given and in a day or so its black beady eyes opened. He eventually started to grab the dropper with both paws and slurp down the warm milk. The fingers would wrap around the bottle just like a baby. Soon he began to walk around the cage and greet us when we would come to him with the milk. Mom named him Buddy Boy. Buddy Boy loved being petted especially on his stomach just like a kitten. He was soft as velvet. He began to climb around the cage during the day chattering and sleeping at night.

Knowing he was a wild animal that belonged outside, we eventually moved the cage to my bedroom next to a window. Buddy Boy grew healthy and bigger. His tail was extremely bushy. Best looking squirrel that I ever did see! Finally, we decided it was time for him to venture outside. We opened my window and his cage to let him outside on top of our porch. At first he walked gingerly on the roof tiles. Every night he would return to his cage to sleep and eat. Gradually, he moved down the porch into the back yard scampering around picking up things to eat. But every night he would return to his nest in my bedroom. We could recognize him from his bushy tail and his chattering.

One weekend we went away. It poured and poured for two days. All we could think about was Buddy Boy and how wet and cold he was. Would he return to us? We didn't know. As our car drove up to the house we could see Buddy Boy on the porch roof waiting for us. I ran in to open the window for him and gave him some milk. He then crawled soaking wet into his cage and went to sleep. When he awoke he was fine and looking to go outside again. We all went on like this for a few months. He would play outside learning to climb trees swinging from the branches and come down to greet us in the back yard to chatter. Every night he would return to his nest in my room.

One weekend my sister came to visit us with her husband and their Basset hound, Beau. As much freedom as we gave to Buddy Boy, he knew no fear playing with the birds, but he had never met a dog. Buddy Boy came down from the trees to examine Beau. Beau attacked him as a hound would and put his mouth around our baby and then dropped him. Buddy Boy was hurt so we called the Vet who said to return him to the cage on the warm blanket. Chances were the dog did not bite the squirrel because the squirrel was distasteful. However, there might be some internal damage from the pressure Beau exerted with his mouth.

We would know in a few days. So we cuddled him and fed him but he stayed lifeless. After a few days, my father and mother took Buddy Boy to the Vet who put him down because of internal injuries. We were very sad.

We learned a lesson which was wild animals belong outside in their habitat where they can learn fear and survival. We thought of Buddy Boy often knowing we had given him life but had naively taken it away.

Pillsbury Dough Boy

I was young when I first married back in 1970 and not very domestic. My cooking abilities were very limited: eggs, sandwiches, and maybe steaks. After our wedding in Washington DC, my husband and I drove to Madison, Wisconsin. He was still in school and I planned to look for a job. The Jewish holidays were approaching and I decided to make a homemade Challah from scratch for Friday night's dinner.

I located all the necessary ingredients at the store and familiarized myself with the baking instructions. Most important was to let the yeast rise two times. I carefully followed the instructions combining the flour, eggs, water, yeast, etc. The mound of dough looked large, but after the allotted time I punched down on it and it gasped. I allowed it to rise again. When the timer sounded, I placed the dough into a pan, rolled, and braided it. An egg wash was next to give the crust shine. The dough was placed into the oven and the door shut. The apartment only had one of those very small one-half size ovens, but I was making do.

After a while, I heard a sound emanating from the kitchen. I went to investigate and to my great surprise the Pillsbury Dough Boy was oozing out the sides of the door which were being pushed open by the bread, and he was also oozing out the top of the door. The bread was raw, inedible, and disgusting. Maybe I did not read the instructions on the yeast pouch well enough. Anyway, we ordered pizza that night.

Remembering the Innocence

My husband and I lived in exurbia before there even was exurbia. We had a nice house on a street with a few other homes and a big farm down the road. Everyone had some property. Innocence seemed all around us with the geese at our back door along with a few ducks and deer running thru our backyard. My step child's, Courtney, 13th birthday was about to happen. As she, through some strategic errors, had become not the most popular girl in her school, I decided to change the situation by giving her the most spectacular birthday party her "friends" had ever taken part in. She lived in Chappaqua, New York which was about an hour ride from our home in Norwalk, Connecticut. She was to invite seven of her friends for an overnight party.

On the appointed day, we picked everyone up and drove them to our house. Immediately I gave everyone huge hats which looked like $33^1/_3$ long play records with lots of crepe flowers on them. First, we had dinner, cake, and ice cream of course. After dinner, Courtney opened her presents. Then I brought out a large box of old clothes and costumes and the girls were to dress up and put on makeup. They were assigned to produce small plays for each other. This went over like gangbusters and took care of a lot of time. My husband kept reminding me that I was not an invited guest and to bow out.

After playtime, my husband and I were getting exhausted so we asked the girls to change into their PJs. Some did and apparently some did not. The next thing we heard was screaming and laughing coming from outside the house toward the street side. Mind you, this was about 12:00 midnight. We ran outside to find the girls in the street waving down cars flaunting their outlandish costumes, etc. The people in the cars were also laughing and enjoying the frolicking girls. We quickly brought the girls into the house and fed them more candy and cake etc. I think they finally went to sleep about 4:00 am laying in their bedrolls all over the living room.

In the morning, we were awakened again by squeals and laughter. We arose knowing it must be breakfast time. Pancakes, eggs, bacon, and toast was served with OJ for nutrition. There was so much syrup you could cut the air with a knife. Reluctantly, the girls packed up asking if they could stay longer. This had definitely been the best party they had ever been to. Peter and I drove them home amidst singing, laughing, and talking. The Thank Yous were profuse. We were pleased that Courtney was the most popular girl in school for the next week or so. Never will we forget the innocence of young girls parading in the street nor their performances in costumes.

Miss-Haps in Japan

The following are two occurrences on my visits to Japan many years ago. Please accept them with a grain of humor. While in Tokyo, I decided to take the Bullet Train to Osaka which would give me a good view of Mount Fuji and the countryside. It is a first class train which travels very fast. I dressed very proper for such a trip - a blouse, slacks, pantyhose, and flat shoes because I was still on business. During the trip, I had to go to the bathroom. Restrooms were easily identified and were unisex. I entered the cubicle and found a porcelain toilet recessed into the floor. There were foot prints on the side pedals. I realized immediately I was in a terrible predicament dressed the way I was, but I had to go. Finally, I slid down my pants, pantyhose, and panties. It was then I realized there was a window from the outside aisle into the cubicle so others could see if the room was occupied. My clothes were entangled around my knees and ankles. At that moment I lost my footing and fell into the bowl. How embarrassing!

On another visit, I took a first time small electronics buyer, Linda Posen from Great Neck, New York with me to Tokyo. She had never been to Asia before. She was young, naïve, with a great sense of humor and had a very husky deep voice that carried well. On the day that we arrived, one of her representatives, Fujimoto-san, toured us around to temples and sights. Toward the end of the afternoon, I told Linda I had a personal stop to make and asked Fujimoto-san to drop me in Shinjuku on a particular street. Linda asked what I was going to do. I explained I had a friend in New York who asked if I would bring back an erotic book from Tokyo so I was going to an erotic bookstore. She said she had never been to one in the States and wanted to join me. When I asked Fujimoto-san to drop us off on a particular street, he grinned and I swear his eyes were smiling. He said he would go into the store with us because it was not safe for women to go alone. When the car arrived at our destination, we got out and went into the store. Linda and I were amazed at the number of books, magazines, and things in the shop. We were the only Caucasians much less women in the store. I proceeded toward the books while Linda went over to some floor to ceiling shelves filled with toys and gadgets. A few minutes later, I heard noises, a thud and hysterical laughter coming from Linda's direction. I found Linda convulsed in laughter. The wall was filled with battery operated sex toys which she had turned on and the entire wall was gyrating, wiggling, and lighting up while some toys were falling on Linda. She was trying to grab the ones falling. Her laugh was so deep, husky, and loud that all of the men were running out of the store shouting Japanese and waving their hands in the air. Fujimoto-san suggested we leave, so we did. I never did get books.

Snap Shots

My company's counterpart in Europe purchased a lot of merchandise from European countries. My job was to ascertain whether there was a market for our stores there. I decided to travel to Europe accompanied by my counterpart in women's and girls' clothing to attend the Prêt a Porte fashion shows. Elaine and I were used to traveling first class in the

Orient. We knew this trip would be different but how different we did not know.

First stop was London for two days. Mario, our representative to England, Italy, and Portugal booked the hotels for us and set up vendor visits. The fashion show and Fair had taken over many of the hotels so rooms were difficult to book. Mario, trying to save our company money, booked us into inexpensive rooms at a top hotel. We each had a room in the back of the hotel on the first floor facing the outside trash cans in an alleyway. Upon entering my very small room, I had to climb over the bed to get into the rest of room. Elaine's room was the same. So much for luxurious accommodations. For the next two days, we visited the show and fairs speaking with various vendors. We took some samples knowing the market was too expensive for us. There was no time for sightseeing, just work.

The next stop was Porto, Portugal and the out region. Again, we visited manufacturers of suits, slacks, and bathrobes. We did not find suitable companies for our business. Mario, a connoisseur of good food and wine took us to wonderful restaurants even if the accommodations were Spartan.

Florence was next. What a wonderful city! Artwork everywhere. Mario was still with us taking us to various vendors at the show. Finally, we told Mario to go home because we wanted a few hours for ourselves. We walked the streets going in and out of stores. We purchased leather clothing and boots for ourselves, and then went to some museums. As we entered one museum, there was Michelangelo's' David. How well endowed he was. The statue was amazing. We saw the Ponte Vecchio Bridge and the Palazzio Vecchio. On our way back to the hotel, a pigeon got my hair and designer jacket. What a mess!

Elaine and I had the weekend off so we decided to go see Venice. It was sleeting and snowing in Venice when we arrived but like mailmen that was not going to stop us. We had booked ourselves into the Hotel

Danieli on Riva degli Schieumi which was amazing, just near Saint Mark's Square and Basilica. Most stores were closed due to the season and the snow. There were lots and lots of pigeons but since the Florence incident I tried to stay out of their way. We took a boat trip to Lido, a resort town, but due to the poor weather we turn around and went back to Venice. We saw the Bridge of Sighs and went museum hopping. In one particular museum there was a group of about twenty Japanese businessmen on a "sex" tour. The leader carried a flag on a stick with him to indicate the group. Japanese tourists were known for these tours. They would go on these tours, do their thing, and then on the last day run around sightseeing and buying gifts for their families. I guess we were one of the sights in the museum. After speaking Japanese to one another, laughing, and carrying on they decided to shock us and "drop trou" (trousers) in front of us. I must tell you, none of them were built like David!

From Venice we next went to Athens, Greece where we met some new representatives. Our hotel accommodations were fine. The dinners primarily consisted of what I called "meet and greet" fish. We were shown to lockers and drawers which were packed with fresh dead fish, all eyes staring up at us. We would select our fish and the restaurants would prepare the fish in the manner we preferred. It was interesting and surprisingly good. Again, we visited factories manufacturing baby clothes, bathrobes, underwear, and fancy girls embroidered dresses. We also visited Thessaloniki. We took samples for testing and had other samples shipped to us. We knew in our hearts that Greece would be a difficult sale to our buyers and stores. The last day we toured the Acropolis, Delphi and other sights by ourselves. On top of Acropolis we found another group of Japanese male tourists. They kept snapping our photos, then giggling and laughing. We suspected what was to come and what we did not want to see again. We walked away, but not fast enough. The trousers came down again. We were not embarrassed, but they should have been.

Our last stop was Tel Aviv. We met up with another representative who had booked us into the Hilton where the fashion show was being held. We roamed the show, spoke with vendors and designers but knew the prices were too high for our market. Finally, a day to ourselves. We toured Tel Aviv and Jerusalem with a driver. In the old part of Jerusalem we saw the Shroud of Turin. What an incredible sight! We saw the Holy City, museums and went to the Wailing Wall. Being of Jewish heritage, I found the Wall and visitors very touching especially all the messages left in the Wall.

The year was 1976 and General Sharon was a bigwig in Israel. At the airport we discovered he and his wife were on our plane. They were big people with booming very boisterous voices and slightly inebriated. Surrounded by body guards, they boarded the plane first. The guards sat all around us protecting the General. We landed at JFK happy to have been to Europe but happier to be home. Our next trip would be back to Asia.

The Chinese Experience

We, in the retail business, were very excited with the announcement by President Nixon to open China for trade with the United States. A new market for inexpensive goods. Only a few business people were allowed into China originally. Business was to be conducted at the Canton Fair where different regions of China would bid for your business. At this time I worked for one of the country's largest retailers in New York City. I was 26 at the time and was a senior international buyer for my company. After a long debate, it was decided I would be one of the first foreign women visitors to China. It was an honor. I was excited and knew I was representing not only my company but also the United States. Lots of inoculations and preparations by my company. The rules required us to travel on two passports because we also had business in Taiwan at the time. China did not recognize Taiwan except as an enemy.

We were required to travel by train via Hong Kong to Quangchou, or Canton as it was known. Although the train ride to the border was only two hours or so, we were stopped at the border, no photos allowed, and given lunch. The lunch lasted about half an hour, but the wait for the connecting train was three hours. All of the travelers ate together, served by indifferent shuffling Chinese in their customary uniforms of grey. Then we sat in the heat, which was horrible, for the next train. It must have been 105 in the shade with very high humidity. They had big ceiling fans which made whirling noises. I was aware of the potential heat and dressed in what I considered conservative clothing, a tee shirt, skirt, and sandals. Finally, the train arrived and we all got on. The seats were wicker and very small, I guess they were made for the Chinese. The Chinese men all smoked these horrible little smelly cigarettes one after another the entire way which thank goodness was only an hour.

It was dark by the time we arrived at the train station. My traveling partner and I hailed a taxi. The taxi raced through the crowded streets with the car lights blinking on and off periodically. Apparently, the taxi drivers turn on the lights when they honked to shoo people away from the intersections. Otherwise, we were driving in the dark and only the sounds of bicycle bells could be heard. We were driving kamikaze style dodging the walkers and cyclists. We finally arrived at the three story hotel called the Tang Fang. We were told to leave our belongings in the lobby and to surrender our passports. We were not alarmed because the Chinese rule was you could leave anything anywhere. Upon your return hours later your belongings would be in the exact place you left them untouched. China was very safe in those days.

It was apparent the hotel was not air conditioned. We were led to our rooms which were extremely small containing a bookshelf, dresser of sorts, and a lumpy single bed with mosquito netting around it. There was a small bath attached. Afterward, I went downstairs to the "dining room" to have a small dinner with my partner. Afterwards we went to "The Top of the Tang Fang" which was air conditioned for Westerners for beer, the only cold drink around. The Germans were already drunk and sloppy from beer and warm hard liquor. No one dared to drink any drink with ice cubes. The water was not safe. The Germans decided to dance to the Chinese music playing and tried to entice me into dancing with them. I begged off.

I was warned to sleep with my camera because my hosts were known to come in at night while people were sleeping and expose the film. I guess they didn't want the outside world to see inside China. I finally decided to go to my room and to bed. I was exhausted. Funny the key didn't seem to do anything in the keyhole but the door was open. It was then I remembered the Chinese do not lock their doors and I guess that meant the same thing for a hotel. I did sleep with my camera.

The next morning I woke up to find my camera, although still in bed with me, had the film exposed. That was a real shock to me. I went into shower and found the shower did not work and the water merely trickled out of the faucet in the tub. I washed my hair anyway with the limited water supply by dunking my head under the faucet. There would be no reason to complain because 1 - There was no one to complain to except the government and 2 - It wouldn't have done any good anyway. This was China, after all, a developing country. I finally left my room and went down to breakfast consisting of a strange type of bread toasted with jam. I couldn't face the congee with a raw egg on top. And tea, of course. I was previously warned about the coffee. It was time to start my day at the fair.

I walked outside and immediately a crowd of Chinese surrounded my partner and me. The Chinese came so close to us it scared me. Some kneeled to look at my legs chattering the whole time in Chinese. It was then I realized most of them had never seen white legs before. The women all wore uniform pants. I purposely did not bring pants thinking I had to look businesslike in my skirt, etc. Little did I realize that I would become a spectacle. It was difficult to walk trying to shuffle the crowd away. Finally, we made it across the street to the Fair. It was very hot, 110 in the shade and all we could drink inside was hot tea which actually cooled the body temperature. We conducted meetings until lunchtime at which time we were invited to lunch by some of our hosts.

Lunch was fabulous - a nine course meal with dishes I had never tasted before and of course, lots of hot tea. We went back to the fair building for more negotiations and hot tea. As the meetings ended early, my partner and I decided to go into the center of the city to go shopping at THE department store. We gathered our flashlights and took a taxi. Daylight riding was as scary as the night time.

We entered the darkly lit store, 15 watt bulbs were sparsely placed. We carried flashlights which helped lead our way pass the counters of goods. Once again, we had crowds surrounding us commenting as we walked. Whenever we came to a counter of interest 25 watt bulbs were lit in the glass enclosures so we could see more clearly. Our purchases fascinated our Chinese followers. They created a sea of grey. All wore grey. After a few purchases we departed. As we walked through the store, the lights behind us would be turned off to save energy but the Chinese crowd kept following us.

Outside we took the same taxi that brought us to the store. The driver had been told to wait for us since taxis were few. Again his horn honked at people everywhere. We passed an outdoor movie theatre where propaganda films were showing. A loud speaker was going in the streets guiding traffic and people on bicycles as well as the walkers. Back to the hotel. In the lobby was a store selling fabulous posters, paintings, gifts, lacquerware, cinnabar jars and plates, stuffed animals made with cat fur, and other arts and crafts. I planned to stop by the next day.

Another hosted dinner was planned for the evening. Again it was nine courses in a very warm restaurant. Fabulous food and, of course, hot tea and Chinese wine. Back to the "Top of the Tang Fang" for some air conditioning and cold beer. The Germans were drunk again and dancing. I finally left and went to bed this time leaving my camera out.

Up again in the morning taking my faucet shower and down to breakfast. Across the street to the Fair where we had two meetings in the morning and then back to the hotel. I shopped at the store in the lobby, went upstairs to pack up, checked out of the hotel, and took a taxi back to the train station. The return trip was much shorter. At the border, our connecting train was waiting. As we departed, I felt like I had been a stranger in a very strange land. And I was.

Mayo Wan Te (which means in Cantonese No Problem)

In Cantonese very often you will hear Mayo Wan Te which means "no problem" to almost everything that is said. I made a lot of good friends overseas while I was working for JC Penney. There was a running joke when some of them saw my significant other, Peter, overseas they would plan a wedding for us. Of course, Peter and I never took them seriously especially since 1 - We never discussed marriage even after three years of living together in New York City and 2 - We never planned for Peter to visit the Far East with me. Besides, there was a rule at work that stated husbands and wives could not travel together overseas.

In 1980, I had received special dispensation from my boss if things were kept quiet so there wouldn't be a backlash from the other buyers, Peter could meet me half way through a nine week trip to Asia in Hong Kong for a weekend. Consequently, on a Friday, Peter joined me on my trip. Friends met him at the airport and transported him to the Sheraton in Kowloon (a city opposite of Hong Kong on the mainland) where he was to meet up with me very late at night. Some other friends got wind and met us at 2:00 am in the lobby. They were ecstatic as this meant they could plan our wedding unbeknown to us. It was a shock when Peter and I realized the wedding they were planning was ours and we had to clarify we really were not getting married. Stunned they asked, "Peter do you love Jane?" and he said, "Yes." And "Jane do you love Peter?" and, I said, "Yes." So they asked immediately, "Then what is the problem?" So, Peter looked at me and asked what should we do? We could post bans and get married or we could forget the entire thing. I thought about it for a moment. Flashing before me was Peter's inability to make decisions, I wasn't getting any younger, he might never ask me again, was I stupid, and finally I said, "Let's do it," within some conditions, however. It must be done on Sunday, my day off, on Bob's junk (Bob was a close friend of ours) in the South China Sea where he is captain and it might be legal, it must be kept very small, quiet, no press, I don't want to know the plans or anything…no involvement on our part. At 2:00 am in the morning I don't think I had ever seen so many elated Chinese all starting to plan my wedding.

"Don't worry, we will plan everything. Mayo wan te - No problem and we will keep the news quiet.

That's what I was afraid, the dreaded mayo wan te.

On Saturday I awoke early for breakfast. The congratulations were circulating within the restaurant. So much for keeping things quiet. I left for work. On Saturday the office shut early, so around 1:00 pm Peter met me. We purchased our wedding bands from the "company" jeweler who, of course, charged us too much but time was of the essence. I showed Peter some of my haunts like Jade Alley and we ate at a noodle kitchen off the main street. Then, back to the hotel room which was covered with flowers and fruit baskets with congratulatory notes. So much for keeping things under wraps. Bob called asking me how many people had I invited onto the junk for the next day. I said no one, we were keeping this small and intimate. I had even wired staff from the other offices not to fly in to see us. He agreed but explained that some mutual friends, buyers at another store, were in town and they would be joining us. We confirmed the pickup time. Bob asked if I was sure no one else had been invited, he was taking a head count for food. I was sure. "Mayo wan te." No problem.

Dinner was provided by some good friends from the industry. It was a lovely twelve course meal including rice birds and shark's fin soup, both delicious. Presents and flowers were lauded upon us. I was a little embarrassed by the gifts and the attention but things are done differently in the Far East and you go with the flow so to speak.

After dinner, I received another phone call from Bob reconfirming how many people had I invited and again I said no one. By now I was getting a little nervous with his Mayo wan tees. Keep it small, Bob. "Mayo wan te."

We met our breakfast date at the Sheraton on Sunday as scheduled. There was a buzz around the restaurant. One or two people mentioned they too were sailing later and maybe we would touch boats. People kept coming by the table congratulating us. Someone said I needed a bouquet of flowers and I should wear a dress for the occasion. All I had was a black sun dress which meant good luck to the Chinese. I selected a few flowers from various arrangements in the room and wrapped them in tin foil to make a tacky arrangement.

At 10:30 am a Rolls Royce limo arrived at the hotel on schedule. We made the rounds picking up food, ice, drinks, etc. and a few guests and then we were on our way to the junk. The junk boy was cursing us under his breath in Chinese about how terrible this event was, it was a mockery of a wedding, etc. None of us listened. On our junk there were approximately 25 folks. Everyone changed into their bathing suits since the wedding wasn't until 3:33 pm Chinese good luck time - lots of time for swimming and sun bathing. Within an hour of arrival to our planned destination spot, a huge yacht tied up to us with at least 150-200 guests on it, many of whom I knew very well. Then small boats tied up along the side much like a flotilla. This was no small wedding. And we were trapped on the South China Sea. Beef Wellington and caviar were served and champagne flowed in glasses on all the boats. Our small improvised wedding took place at 3:33 with Bob presiding over us. Bans had been posted but the legality would still be questioned. Who cares about the paperwork on this gorgeous sunny day on the South China Sea on a Chinese junk! It was romantic and at least the wedding was confined to those who arrived on the boats, a mere 250 or so.

The chairman of my office stood up and then after congratulating us announced Peter and I would need to leave Hong Kong since the rules clearly indicated husbands and wives could not travel together overseas. He could turn an eye if we were in another country but not if we stayed where he was stationed. No problem. We were leaving in the morning for Thailand. Mayo wan te.

After dashing off a brief telex to my New York boss just to let him know what transpired on my day off on the South China Sea, covering my butt, we left for Bangkok. We had managed to keep things as quiet as possible, so we thought. What we didn't know was that morning the newspapers apparently ran stories about this crazy American couple who married on the South China Sea. Good thing we were gone. On our last night in Bangkok while walking around the pool at the Oriental, a lady came running up to us, "Wow, you're the couple who got married in Hong Kong. I was at your wedding. You don't know me but I was on the big yacht and I told all of my friends about it." So much for keeping things small and quiet!

"Mayo wan te." No problem.

Sahwadee

My husband, Peter, and I were married on a junk on the South China Sea outside of Hong Kong in a very impromptu wedding. We flew to Bangkok afterwards as I had business in a factory, but other than that this was to be a quiet respite for us. We stayed at the Oriental Hotel which had its own rich history. We were invited out to dinner the first night. Kondo-san, a Japanese businessman, took us to a Geisha House as in his opinion they had the best food. In a private dining room, the Geisha hostess entered in a very seductive flowered kimono. She poured green tea and served us drinks. Kondo-san knew I was very fond of sashimi, raw fish usually without any rice. The hostess then brought in a three foot tray with a fish made of ice chips. It was covered with sashimi cut into pieces to form the design of the fish. Peter and I were delighted and started our dinner with Kondo-san. After we were satiated with the fish, the hostess brought in the actual dinner. Apparently the fish was the appetizer but since we had gorged on the fish we were not hungry. We ate anyway so as not to lose face in front of our host. "Losing face" is what happens when you are embarrassed or have done something to offend someone else. He then discussed the chopstick holders at each plate. They were white porcelain female nude bodies. On the bottom of each one was a name of a female that was to be partnered with each man. Peter's was Kiki, but we never did meet her. When dinner was over we returned to the hotel.

 The next morning we were picked up by Kondo's car and taken to the factory on the outskirts of Bangkok. The buildings were surrounded by fences and large gates. We drove thru the gates. There were turrets in each corner of the protected area but who were they protecting? There were machine guns and rifles in the turrets, some pointed outside to stop rebels from entering the compound, but other guns were pointed to the inside to keep the factory workers inside. Inside the compound, we saw the dormitories for the workers and large cafeterias. We drove by car to a large building and were asked to get out to enter into the main office. Inside Kondo-san greeted us, served tea, and we talked about business. He proceeded to show me lightweight jackets that he produced for other customers in the United States, Europe, and Canada.

Peter liked one of them and I asked our host for a sample. He agreed and then we took a tour of the factory to see the production which Peter found fascinating as they were weaving flannel cotton for linings from cotton yarn. Back in the states, Peter's factory made velour in much the same way for his powder puffs. After the tour, Kondo-san gave me the sample jacket, we returned to the car and were driven back to the hotel. In the car I examined the jacket and found Kondo stamped SAMPLE on the back of it and mutilated one sleeve so he didn't have to use his export quota. What a cheapskate! Peter and I laughed.

That night we were escorted to a seafood restaurant famous for its blue lobsters. There were 15 of us celebrating our marriage. Our hosts were mainly Japanese and Thai so there was a lot of drinking. Dinner was preordered. First there were appetizers, then a dinner with various Thai delicacies. We were warned not to get too stuffed because the Piece de Resistance was still to come. The servers then brought out a long board totally garnished. In the center was a blue lobster at least five feet long with no claws. Fifteen of us ate on that one lobster.

The next day was my day off so we decided to go sightseeing. First was a motorboat taxi ride along the Chao Phraya River. It runs north and south throughout the city. The Thai bathe, wash their clothes, drink, pee, and defecate in the river. It is central to many lives. Any splashing requires you to immediately wipe off the rancid water. We traveled past unbelievable slums and magnificent homes juxtaposed to each other.

First was a visit to the Grand Palace on the river bank. Outside the palace are the And Wat Phrakaew (Emerald Buddha) and the Wat Po (Giant Reclining Buddha). A Wat is a Thai temple. These temples were exotic and amazing. As we walked around, we found many houses had miniature Wats outside of them hanging like mailboxes.

One of the more impressive temples to us was the Teapot Temple which is made up of embedded pieces of teapots and cups with handles. We found the design amusing because the Thai drink from cups without handles but we saw a lot of handles in the walls. It was a statement about the British colonization. We visited at least 25 major Wats that day until I was "Wat-ted" out.

We took a regular taxi to a shopping area. We shopped for silks and antiques. Many items sold as antiques are not. The Thai are known to take a new object, bury it into the ground, and wait for it to look old. Then it is called an antique.

Exhausted, we started back to the hotel. A young man stopped us to practice his English. Peter became leery when the man tried to touch me with his left hand. That is absolutely taboo and an insult in Thailand because men eat with their right hand and wipe their behinds with their left if you know what I mean. I thought Peter was going to slug him so I whisked him down the street toward the hotel.

Tired, we returned to the hotel and enjoyed an intimate and quiet dinner for our last night. We reflected on our amazing, fascinating, and exotic experience. We realized how fortunate we had been to see this part of the world.

Camping

During our third year of marriage, my husband and I decided to go on a camping detour on our way to San Francisco. He when to South Dakota and met up in Colorado where we rented a car and went west. Having never camped before, we packed a pop tent in which to sleep. Looking at the map we selected a state park.

We stopped and set up the tent. Having never set up a tent before one side kept collapsing. Finally, we worked it out. No one else seemed to be in the camping area. There was a hole in the ground for building a fire.

We decided to go into town, find a butcher, and buy a steak and some potatoes. Upon returning, we gathered some wood and built a fire. The steak and potatoes were incredibly fresh and delicious.

As dusk descended upon us, the stars appeared. Coming from New York City, we were mesmerized by their brightness. The entire sky was filled with thousands of stars.

Finally, we crawled into the tent to go to sleep. Something was crawling around the tent. Using our flashlights, we found a medium sized snake staring at us. Neither one of us knew the difference between snakes with poison and friendly ones. After getting the beast out of our tent, we secured the sides to the ground with rocks so no others would enter into our little domain. We were freaked. All night we listened for sounds, wolves, and coyotes, etc.

In the morning we awoke, got dressed, decided to pack up and go out for breakfast. As we packed up, we found another snake, this time a much larger snake wiggling around. Totally scared we ran to the car, locked the doors, and took off. Outside the park, I glanced at the map to determine which way to go next. We quickly discovered the camping site where we had spent the night was called "Snake Canyon." We did not wonder why.

Island on the Equator

During my travels, I visited Sri Lanka, an island once known as Ceylon, several times. It is hot and dusty with many coconut trees sitting in the Indian Ocean on the Equator. The last time that I was there, I was five months pregnant but looked eight or nine months. The custom's official demanded to go through all of my luggage (five bags of clothing and samples) until I bribed him with a pack of American cigarettes. Then he passed me through with no problem. I was met at the airport by a good friend, Ramchand, who owned a factory in Colombo. I was booked into "THE" deluxe western hotel. My room overlooked the train tracks and the view allowed me to observe the passengers and cargo on the trains. Never had I seen so many dusty and ragged people squashed into the cars and hanging out the windows like locusts.

That evening I went to Ram's home which by Colombo standards was a mansion. It had tall walls surrounding it with gates large enough for cars to enter. We sat in his courtyard and had drinks while the rats played and ran across the yard. Finally around nine o'clock I asked about dinner. Dinner was back at my hotel because it was known for its quality and service. The women who served were thread thin even emaciated looking and wore ill-fitting white shirts with black skirts. Everything we ate, shrimp, steak, salad dressing, everything had been cooked or soaked in coconut oil. The smell was noxious and barely edible but I tried not to gag and ate a little. Afterwards, I said goodnight and retired to my room.

In the morning I went downstairs to breakfast. I was so hungry that I ordered waffles and bacon since what can anyone do to waffles? To my surprise they were cooked in coconut oil and even the butter had a coconut flavor. I used pure cane syrup which also tasted strange to my taste buds. Everything in the country seemed to be cooked and steeped in coconut oil except for the tea. From then on, I only ordered toast and jam to keep from heaving.

That day I went to Ram's office and factory in his car where the workers manufacture flannel shirts. The workers wore uniforms as in so many countries I visited. They import the cotton flannel from other countries but cut and sew the shirts in the facility. I generally ordered 500,000 shirts from them and was there to increase the order since the quality was so good. Ram insisted I select some raw silk from his store so he could have a sari made for me to bring home to wear after I had the baby. After the factory tour I was presented with my gift and a blouse to go with the sari.

Later in the day I met up with an old friend, Adil, a Pakistani, who now lived in Colombo. He wanted to show me the Indian Ocean at dusk. We drove to the beach and parked. The beach was crowded with a mass of humanity all walking around and watching the sunset. Colombo is on the Equator and the view is a complete semi-circle of ocean unlike our sunsets which are horizontal. The world is truly round. We watched as the full moon rose. What an incredible sight. As we turned to go back to the car we realized a crowd had surrounded us. Adil had to push people aside so we could walk. At some point, some of the peasant women started shoving and throwing their children and babies at me. Most were maimed and a few seemed to be lifeless. Adil later explained to me these women are beggars and they purposely maim and kill their children so visitors feel sympathy and give them money for food. I was sick to my stomach. Never had I seen that side of inhumanity before. I asked to return to my hotel where I had toast and jam and retired for the night.

The next day I was driven to the airport. All I could think about was the difference between the "haves" and "have nots" was so great. It was beyond my naïve comprehension.

Animal House

My son, Geoffrey, was only five when he realized we lived in an animal house in Connecticut. He was amazed other families did not have such "normal" animals. We had Puppy, the cat, so named as he would bark like a dog. Aside from being the "supercat" flying off his cat house with a sock hanging in his mouth to my bed, he had another unique ability. He would lay on the television upside down and chase football players on the screen with his paws. He was usually more entertaining than the game.

Then there was Bonnie, a Brindle bull dog. Aside from looking like a pig and snorkeling around, Bonnie became the favorite at soccer games. During half time, we would release her from her leash and she would run onto the field, kicking and mouthing the soccer ball while playing with the children. After halftime, the ball would be covered in drool.

Mousemeat, the cat, was known for catching mice in the basement which was great until she laid the dead mice on my stomach as I slept. She was so proud of herself.

You could not look at Benji, our Bedlington terrier, straight in the eyes. His eyes were on the side of his head, much like a flounder. He was also groomed like a baby lamb. Being a terrier, he liked to chase wild animals around our yard, like hedgehogs and squirrels. He just gawked at the wild turkeys because of their size and squawking. We had an electric fence which he could jump and run through without getting shocked while pursuing animals. Very often we would hear him barking only to realize that he could not get back into the yard. If he ambled back, he would hear and feel the shock of the fence and would not cross it. Very often we would have to go out and take off his collar so he could come back home.

Our eldest son, Matt, gave Geoffrey a pet snake for his birthday. The snake roamed his tank and ate frozen dead mice that Matt would feed him. One day, Geoff reported that the snake was not eating or moving. We went upstairs to his bedroom only to find that the snake had committed "snakeacide" by tying himself into a knot. We definitely had an animal house filled with loving pets we adored.

Mr. Kim

I met Mr. Kim Sang when he first visited New York City in 1976 to promote his company to our buyers. He was president of his company, a multi-million dollar conglomerate in Korea. Customarily, vendors would wine and dine the buyers. Our company policy stated that we should reciprocate once in a while. I never knew anyone who did, but I did. I wanted to show my appreciation to them. Kim and I had an immediate rapport. Everyone knew I was a little kooky. I decided to show Kim a side of New York he would probably never see again so I decided to take him to The Feast of San Janero in Little Italy with booths, eateries, and games. A true New York event.

I picked up Kim at his hotel and asked if he was game for this. He said, "Of course," I hailed a taxi and down we went to Little Italy. The cab driver, thinking we were both foreigners decided to take a longer route. I had a fit, excused myself to Kim, and then told the driver off in no uncertain terms. From then on he took the short cuts.

We arrived amidst the Christmas type lights, loud music, and neon signs. Kim was immediately taken by the sights of various food booths, games, hawkers, and crowds. We strolled through the streets eating, gambling, and shopping for small items. He actually won at the games and gave me a stuffed animal. I kept asking if this was okay with him and he smiled saying the festival was great. We dined in a small Italian restaurant known for its food where a king of the mafia was murdered. This was quite an experience for Kim. In fact, during his subsequent interviews with the buyers he spoke about it. They were shocked that I would take such an important man to the festival but I knew that he had participated in a real part of New York not just an expensive uptown restaurant. He had a good time and we were bonded for life because I had treated him like a regular person with a lot of respect.

Each time he visited we would go out and talk for hours usually in the presence of his Korean staff.

Each time I visited Seoul I would call him on the phone and say, "Yobo asayo" which meant "Sweetie, Hello." He would always respond in Korean and I'd say "Stop stop. It's Jane," then we would laugh. He would take my staff, his staff, my future husband and myself out to wonderful restaurants. This special relationship continued for years.

In Seoul, he introduced me to his antique dealer and I purchased a Korean medicine chest and an old Japanese armoire left over from the Japanese occupation of Korea. The same night Kim invited me out to dinner and dancing with John, the head of my Korean office. We danced closely with each other with memories of what should and could have been. Knowing this could never be, I just married, he with a family. I had helped to elevate his company to a world status; he gave to me good conversation and friendship. Our bodies co-mingled and our legs were intertwined. We had tremendous feeling and respect for one another.

A few years later, Kim became very ill and was aging ungracefully from a disease ravaging his body. He came to see me at my hotel for breakfast for one last meeting. He appeared rather frail and thin, a mere shadow of himself from the days of yore, a warrior still fighting for his place in life. He announced to me that he had always loved me and wanted me to know before his last days on earth. I intended to go to his funeral in Seoul but John advised me it wouldn't have been proper. I will always remember my special times with Kim.

Kowtow Kowloon - "Traditional Kowloon"
I have always enjoyed learning about other cultures, people, values and customs. Working for a major retailer afforded me an opportunity to visit other countries and people before they became ultra-westernized. In my free time on the trips, I would walk the streets in and out of neighborhoods observing people living their daily lives, going to bazaars, eating in strange restaurants, shop and barter. If your eyes are open to new experiences then you can absorb and learn a lot.

Kowloon Territory is across the Lei-Yue Mun Straight from Hong Kong and looks into the New Territories and countryside. Back in the late 1970s and 1980s it contained The Walled City, Kowloon Peninsula and New Kowloon. The Walled City was originally a Chinese military fort with 33,000 people within a 6.5 acre area. Previously, the city was controlled by the Triads with high rates of prostitution, gambling, and drug use. Demolished in the early 1990's, a public park was built. Back then most of Kowloon was a cosmopolitan area of 4.97 million people per one square mile. That is and was a lot of people in a very small area.

Owned and governed by Great Britain at the time it became infamous for lawlessness and squalor. Many called it anarchy as few police entered the area. Peace was kept by friendly gangs. Today it has 18 districts and is governed by the Mainland Chinese. The major street in Kowloon is Nathan Road which runs south and north and begins at the Peninsula Hotel, an infamous five star hotel, which is where I stayed.

I would often walk up Nathan Road, about one mile, away from the tourist and hotel region. I saw high rise buildings being erected with scaffolding made of bamboo sticks. It was amazing these edifices could withstand the typhoons which were common in the area. I observed tenements with laundry hanging out the windows, daycare centers, and stores juxtaposed in an interconnected web of 14 story skyscrapers with no regard to architects or planners. The first McDonalds was built in the late 1970s serving the regular menu plus several Chinese dishes. The lines to get into it were wrapped around for blocks. Off the main street was a maze of narrow alleys which resembled a mouse maze. The alleys were developed in part as protection against thieves who had no easy escape could be readily caught. I walked past bakeries, jewelry, grocery, meat stores, and restaurants. Finally, I arrived at my destination alley. The entrance was covered with neon signs. Quickly I realized I was the only guilow (foreign devil) around. I walked past stalls of ivory, jewelry, electronics, fake watches, and small restaurants. The aroma emanating from the eateries permeated the air. I would enter a particular noodle shop and eat. Then I would walk into the jostling alley again. The alley was old, needing much repair and painting and was very dirty.

"Any watch 25 dollar." I negotiated prices on a few things using hand signals and paper since I didn't speak Chinese. I offered $5 for a fake Rolex. He said, "No". I offered two watches for $10. He said okay and I selected the two I wanted and walked on. Monks, peasants, and the well-heeled were all visiting the stalls.

The prices were significantly lower than the tourist areas. I would walk to the Chinese Department Store where I could buy products from China very inexpensively, such as cashmere sweaters, blankets, bee balm jelly used for increasing the male libido, various herbal remedies, and vitamins. I stuffed my purchases into a large tote bag. Then I walked to Jade Alley where roughly a hundred vendors sold and traded jade, fake jade, and jadite jewelry, stones, and decorative arts. Tourists would visit the market to find bargains.

"Any piece 25 dollar." Again I offered $5. "Business no good, okay." All I can say is, "Buyers beware!" you never really know what you were buying!

I would keep walking until I reached the old walled section and then turn around and walk back to my hotel which was a long way. I refused to take the rickshaws thinking it was a demeaning job for very poor and usually old men. As I entered the tourist area again, I became aware I was no longer the only Caucasian. Exhausted, I entered the hotel and went up to my room in the safe confines of four walls. What I didn't know then was the "floor boys" would place a match in the door jams. The match would fall down if the door was opened. In this way they could keep track of your comings and goings.

I had been to a part of Kowloon few visitors ever saw. I had been a "stranger in a strange land" and feeling fortunate to have seen Kowloon before modernization had taken place.

Only Your Own Teeth Need Apply

After being alone for many years my therapist suggested for me to enter the dating world. What? Me? At my age? I guess I can try the computer senior dating scene. Others do. What would I say? Do senior people lie or exaggerate on the apps like the under 30 crowd? Lots of things have changed since I last dated. In the past, I was always wary of lies in a man's description of himself and now there is Viagra. What does that

WORLD TRAVELER

say about a man? He could lie about raw emotions? Sexual diseases are rampant in the over 50 crowd. Do most women think we are too old to get STD's? Is he retired or on disability? Where are the nice guys? Not the gigolos from Aruba. Not the sexual animals but ones interested in long term relationships. Let's take a closer look at one particular ad.

"63 year-old good looking retired senior in good shape, loving, not religious, caring, mellow, individual who enjoys gardening, reading, TV, movies, restaurants, cooking, working out, and the beach and who is looking for a long term relationship. I have a dog, no children, like to travel to warm climates, am a casual smoker (a few times a week), and own a house. I am into 'oldie' music and cars."

What, did a woman write this? Everyone says they go to the movies, they read, and they want a long term relationship so these are throw away lines.

Is he really 63? Everyone lies about their age. What if he is really 70? I don't care about the age, but it is the lying I wonder about. What are his wrinkles really hiding? Or are they really crinkles? Which is worse wrinkles or crinkles?

Good looking is a relative term. The Munsters probably thought they were good looking too. Mellow? Does he still get high on marijuana or something else? Is he a pill junkie? Who knows?

He does have a nice smile according to the darkened photo. Are those his own teeth? Well, they are if he paid for them. He has lots of hair which could be transplants. So what am I left with when I pick apart this ad? A 70 year-old hippie who has hair transplants, has false teeth, could have a beer belly which is hidden by his Florida type shirt unbuttoned down to the middle of the chest wearing gold chains and probably Bermuda shorts. His devotion to his dog replaces his need for a child. I understand the symbiotic relationship but there is a difference between giving bones and a boner. He lives alone in a hermit existence watching TV, renting movies, dieting, and working out. Thrifty or cheap, he owns two old cars that are probably in need of constant repair and they may reflect on his life spending. He lives in a house and does some gardening enough to keep up appearances. He cooks because, if he didn't, he wouldn't eat sometimes. It doesn't mean he is creative in the kitchen. He travels most likely to Florida, is a chain smoker, nonreligious (deletes that as a problem) and goes to various restaurants but only if he has the appropriate coupons.

Or

He could be a 63 year-old good looking man in decent shape, has his own teeth and hair, who is loving, caring, etc. Never had children, but loves animals, enjoys going to the movies and restaurants. Enjoys being be adventurous in cooking using herbs and vegetables from his garden. He enjoys warm weather and beaches especially in North and South Carolina as well as the Caribbean islands. The photo was taken in Hawaii thus the printed shirt. He is well traveled. Comfortable with "oldie" music and he plans to purchase a new car soon. He does smoke occasionally. Nonreligious based on prior experiences.

Two interpretations of the same bio. Will I chance going out on the senior network or will I be so stymied? In the end what does it really matter? If he has a good heart, if he is truthful, if we enjoy the same things, has a beer belly, false teeth and/or balding: Bring him on! After all, someone is picking apart my bio also.

The Secret Attacker - Lyme Disease

The deer, the chipmunks, the squirrels, aren't they cute in our yards, on the condo property scampering all around us. They would be cuter to me if I didn't know they were transferring the dreaded Lyme disease to Leisure World residents and our pets. I think we could be in the middle of another epidemic of Lyme. Temperatures, headaches, muscle pain, lethargy, sleep disorder, vision problems, nerve damage, and memory disorders. Decreased concentration, chills, joint pains, sexual disorders, bi-polar, depression, emulating fibromyalgia and arthritis (shall I go on?) it can be difficult to diagnose. It can elude even the basic tests which is why a person must be vigilant in his search at times. Lyme Disease is an inflammatory disease which is spread through a tick bite initially. I have listed above the possible counter indications of a bite. They are far reaching. The long term effects can be inflammation, Lyme arthritis, heart rhythm, and nervous system problems. Ehrlichiosis or babesiosis may develop. Ehrlichiosis is spread by the deer tick bite and is similar to Rocky Spotted fever and typhus. The red blood cells are covered by a single parasite which is spread to humans by ticks in Babesiosis which is less common and usually requires hospitalization.

Leisure World residents are unprepared for the onslaught of tick bites that have and will occur. The familiar bull's eye rash doesn't always appear as a warning to us. When it does, the rash is usually a textbook indication of the bite but when it doesn't appear that is when the patient develops a problem in diagnosing Lyme. Worse yet, Lyme can stay in the system for years without detection. A person can contract it gardening, hiking, walking your dog, playing bocce ball, or doing lots of mundane things outdoors. The tick is so tiny it is difficult to see much less find unless it is engorged with blood. The best protection is to wear socks, long pants and long sleeves when walking or doing outdoor activities. Leisure World has never had so many deer and therefore so many Lyme ticks. Small animals, rodents and birds spread the ticks and Lyme after being bitten.

We have become complacent about Lyme thinking that it is on the wane. The truth is it is not. The basic tests do not necessarily tell the facts. New information coming to light indicates more expansive and extensive tests may be needed to detect Lyme. When looking at the list of masquerading illnesses, one must realize how difficult Lyme can be to diagnose. If you have any of the sustaining illnesses above and cannot find a cure, you might want to investigate the Lyme possibility. At least, rule it out.

Why am I so interest in Lyme? Why do I know so much? My son contracted Lyme when he was very young. For years it went without diagnoses because it masqueraded as Multiple Sclerosis, diabetes, and many other illnesses. And now that we finally know what he has, it is incurable and he will be on meds or in and out of hospitals for the rest of his life fighting the tick that bit him or bit me during my pregnancy.

Guardians of the House

I inherited Timmy, a tuxedo cat and he has finally adopted me three years later. We tend to think that we select our pets but honestly I think they select us. I went to a rescue home and found Jade. She was a black fluff ball and a white spot on her belly with amber eyes. She immediately came over to me foregoing her brothers and sisters and that was it. We became partners immediately. I took her home and after a few days she acclimated to the house and to Timmy, my other cat. She answers to anything similar to Jade, Jadite, Jadie, etc. She will greet me at the door much like a dog will do, meowing, welcoming me home. Jade has her own bed and hiding places but her favorite place at night is my bed after everyone has gone to sleep. When it is lights out she travels the entire house checking all of the doors to make sure they are shut and locked and checks all of the lights. Timmy, on the other hand, goes to bed with me, sleeps on my pillow and at some point he switches to the bottom of the bed near my legs.

With leaps and bounds Jade jumps onto my bed, curls up, and goes to sleep for awhile. Later she will climb up on me and we will share breaths. I think this began when I had pneumonia and she did not know whether I would pull through or not so she constantly checked to make sure I was still breathing. When she sensed a problem, she would go get my roommate for help and he would give me medicine or change my position, etc. I swear she helped to pull me through. To this day she still checks me.

Timmy spends his days and nights on top of the dining room table. When he is not there he is hiding behind the curtains near the window where he can take in all of the action outside. Timmy's problem is he snores very loudly and gives him away at any given time. Making some friends in the neighborhood has involved Jade sitting in her favorite plant near the window and some deer will come up to it daily at dusk. They share glances and communicate. Then there is her favorite frog playing on the window at night in the shadows of the lamplight. She paws the window and he dances back and forth.

Jade has her favorite TV shows. Every Tuesday at 7:30 pm she watches and listens to Maryland Outdoors. She enjoys the birds and sounds, tilting her head and meowing. The hunting season especially intrigues her because she has not figured out how and why the birds and ducks drop down from the sky. She reaches out to the football players during the games trying to help the players make touchdowns. Late at night, she particularly enjoys David Letterman with his diving dogs and stupid dog tricks. Timmy perceives the TV as background noise much like a radio. It keeps him company.

Particularly finicky when it comes to Jade's diet, I guess she takes after me in this respect. She and her pal, Timmy, share two types of dry food on demand and twice a day they get a wet dinner. If I do not feed her the correct wet food she will snub her nose up at it and walk away pouting and tear through the house really upset knocking everything in her path. Scratching at the furniture comes into play at that point. I get upset and use the squirt water bottle which does not help the situation. It is best to feed her what she likes to avoid a time of crisis. Timmy eats everything including people food. He is partial to butter, clams, and chicken. We actually fight over chicken.

Jade and Timmy are indoor cats. The few times they have gotten out have been exhilarating for them. They check out every inch of the patio, chasing moths, playing with ants, and hiding in the bushes etc. Once or twice Jade has gotten out got of "the pen" and has found me gardening on the side of the house. Proud of herself for finding me she sat very quietly watching my every move until I noticed her. After I properly identified her, I carried her onto the patio where she jumped and ran toward the house as if to say, "I know where I live, do you?"

Not thrilled with strangers, Jade will stay hidden until she feels it is safe to come out of hiding. If Timmy goes out and communicates it is okay then slowly Jade will skulk and then head for her food area first to make sure it is still there. If everything is fine then she will start to relax and greet the visitors. If things are not okay she will misbehave, heading for the couch first by kneading and picking at it, and then tearing through the living room.

Timmy and Jade are cats and have informed us of our place in the house and how they want to be treated. On the other hand, they have helped us which they never let us forget. They are truly the Guardians of the House.

Quack! Quack!

George lives with me and we ride the buses in Leisure World a lot. We know the bus drivers and most of the passengers very well. Jokes abound on the rides and we laugh. Of course we are the butt of many jokes as we are known as the "First Couple."

The other day, George got on the bus at our stop and the driver asked where I was. He answered I was at a meeting with my boyfriend. So the driver asked if the man was really my boyfriend. George replied, "Back home in the Virginia we used to say, if it looks like a duck, walks like a duck, quacks like a duck then it must be a duck." The driver and the entire bus of riders laughed until their bellies hurt.

WORLD TRAVELER

The next day, there was a different driver. Usually when we get on the bus there is talking, etc. This day there was not a sound on the bus. You could hear a pin drop. George got on the bus and sat behind the driver which is where he usually sits. Things were too quiet. As he sat down and the bus began to move, then he heard from all of the riders in unison, "QUACK! QUACK!" Then everyone including George laughed and laughed.

The bus riders really are a community.

♦ ♦ ♦ ♦ ♦

About the Author

Jane was born in Chicago. She moved with the family to Washington DC, Virginia, and eventually settled in Montgomery County, Maryland. She graduated from Montgomery Blair High School and then attended the University of Wisconsin, Maryland and Hunter College in New York majoring in Communications, Television, and Radio.

She worked in Manhattan's Garment Center in the early stages of the import clothing industry. Eventually, she was employed by a major retailer as a coordinator and Senior International Buyer. She has lectured and traveled extensively. After President Nixon opened China to trade, Jane was one of the first women to be allowed into the country.

Married for the second time in 1980 in the South China Sea outside of Hong Kong, Jane and her husband moved to Connecticut where they had a son, two dogs, and three cats. They operated three golf shops on Long Island. She also marketed Mutual Funds. After becoming disabled with a back injury, she moved to Charleston, South Carolina, to walk the beach in recovery. Jane returned to Maryland to be with her mother in Leisure World.

CHAPTER 8

A Student for Life

By Marion Bedell

The Test

It is not easy to take a college entrance exam, especially at age 43, while living with two college student sons who already went through the experience. I was not going to tell a soul, not even my family. I did not want to be embarrassed in case I failed. The probability was strong.

My weakest subject was Math. I silently started practicing the multiplication tables and gave myself imaginary problems to solve. Numbers kept going round and round in my thoughts, while I shopped, prepared and served dinner, and cleaned the house. My husband began to suspect something when he came home for dinner and asked what I did all day. "Twenty-seven times," I answered with a faraway look in my eyes.

"What? Twenty-seven times," he worriedly asked.

"Oh nothing," I answered with a desperate attempt at nonchalance. Darn it, why couldn't I just give quick flippant replies without revealing myself. I break out with nervous beads of perspiration on my face if I so much as think of lying.

The truth finally came out at dinner after my son asked me about the easiest way to get to Macys and I told him to divide it by three. My husband wanted to know if I had swallowed the calculator. I seemed to be number happy. It was a relief to tell the truth. I really did need their help and expertise in math. However, what was not needed was their philosophical, sophisticated encouragement.

"Don't worry Mom," my 19 year-old counseled me, "It's not as if your life's work depends on you being accepted. You always have Dad to support you and half of your life is almost over anyway. Your house keeping and child rearing was great, even without a college degree."

He was judging and grading me before I even took the exam. "Thank You," I muttered while trying to decide whether or not I had received a compliment. Later my 21 year-old took me aside for a sincere confidential down-to-basics talk. "Mom," he started, "You are 43 years old." (There were those numbers again.) This was one number I did not need drilling on. "You are going to be competing with very hip young people." (Did I look like I needed a cane?) "Who," he continued, "have been consistently using their minds." Of course, I sarcastically thought, according to society, my brain went dormant the moment I got married.

My son then calmly inquired as to what I was planning to major in, if I was accepted. This conversation had overtones of something I had listened in on only a couple of years ago. He tried to explain that I had housework and would not be able to handle more than 12 credits per semester, probably less. It will take more than five years to graduate. (There were those dreadful numbers again.)

"You will be 48 by the time you graduate," he exclaimed, "You will be almost 50." I was not that bad in math not to realize that two years just integrated into nothing. "And a Master's degree is required for most teaching positions," my un-encouraging son advised me, "You will be practically ready to retire before you start teaching." Multiplication sure happens fast when years are concerned.

My husband's advice was more practical, "Don't forget to take your reading glasses when you take the exam."

That evening I sat them all down for a pre-college talk. Whether I go to college now or not, I will still reach the age of 48, 49, 50, and with God's help will continue to grow by numbers whether you multiply, add, divide, or subtract. What do I have to lose? I might gain something. This was now beginning to sound like a profit and loss statement.

"You are right, Mom," they conceded, "You go and have a good time. Only please try not to be in any of my classes." According to their thinking I was going to a party while their studies was serious work. However, they promised to help out with household duties and I sure will hold them responsible for that agreement.

Flight from Life - Part Time

"Don't you have anything else to do besides daydream?" "Don't just sit around staring into space!" "Do something. Idle hands lead to idle minds." These were my mother's renowned, reprimanding proverbs whenever she caught me at my favorite pastime: daydreaming.

My guilt feelings of wasting time are still with me. But I must admit that some of my happiest moments are spent daydreaming. I was never very good at any one thing in particular but in my fantasies I become unequaled. The mundane life becomes exciting, intriguing, and shocking. This is not an easy task. Daydreaming is an art that must be cultivated under certain conditions to achieve the maximum satisfaction. Both the topic and a proper locale are important.

For instance through my readings on vacation last summer I became fascinated with Egypt. I know I would have made a terrific Cleopatra. And so, my book drops into my lap, my eyes take on a see nothing, yet knowledgeable glassy stare and I exit from this world of realities. I dream away to my heart's content.

Seductively attired while sitting on my bejeweled, golden throne, on my ornate barge, I slowly glide down Lake George. Instead of pyramids at the water's edge I have luscious green foliage. I can easily go as fast or as slow as desired because my barge is motorized. (Ha, Cleopatra could not do that.) All the boaters and bathers become my adoring peasants who stand and gape in unbelievable awe at the magnificence and at the splendor floating before them. I am the star in my self-directed, self-appointed drama. The sun and my golden barge disappear together, thereby ending a most enjoyable retreat. Lake George has become as exciting as the Nile.

Another favorite daydream (again going back in time) is becoming the first famous female artist. My rendition of Sunflowers was like no other ever. The critics were shocked at my daring to be different. My use of color made Van Gogh's painting look dull. A radiance emitted from my flowers struck the viewer with an almost indecent emotional impact. People began lining up at the Louvre and waiting for hours in pouring rain just to view my creations.

When the plumbing breaks down and the frustration of being the weaker sex becomes overwhelming, is the signal to forge ahead into my science-fiction daydream where the other sex rules. In this world, certain obligatory tasks are automatically performed by the muscular dominating male. In the future dream-world, the female will not have to wear the mask of pleading helpless femininity, nor use cunning guile to get the pipes fixed. The task will be performed simply because she is the master of what should be done, and when.

Guilt feelings force me to justify the temporary escape from the world by daydreaming. It is simply the most enjoyable way to have fun and laugh. Depending on a person's mood daydreaming can either be sophisticated or dumb, a tragedy or a comedy, or a murder mystery. It makes up for being born too late or too soon, for being too tall or too short. It is one of the few enjoyable happenings that is still free. Perhaps I'll write a book on "How to Daydream."

Love? or Not!

His words say he is sorry.
His actions display anger.
Is love in the actions or the telling?

Is negative action mean?
Is no action love?
Can nothing be something?
Where is the dream?

Happenings evolve from feelings.
Feelings evolve from a need.
And the thought is discovered.
Action then becomes the seed of love.

Secrets

It cannot reproduce,
    It cannot grow,
It lacks a heart,
    But can put on a show.

To touch the smooth exterior
    will leave your fingertips cold.
While emotions are varied:
    Shown only to the bold.

Its color shines
    Like a chunk of ice.
Yet catches the sunshine
    Throws it back.
Oh so nice.

The world is watched
    With a glassy stare
That can lighten and brighten
    everywhere.

It will reveal the fact
    without any tact.
It sees all, knows all, and reveals all.
    My mirror on the wall.

The Decorator

She lived on the 27th floor of a luxurious high rise building in New York City. The white carpet was four inches thick, making you feel as though you were walking on clouds. The off-white silk couch curved around one corner of the living room. On the large wall hung an original-sized copy of Matisse's abstract "Dancing Figures." Another wall displayed Picasso's "Face of a Lady," showing both sides of her face on the same canvas. Also hanging was the colorful yet grotesque face of "Woman" painted by Willem de Kooning. She was proud of the progress of her decorating skills.

The dining room wall, however, was still blank. She had searched every art gallery in the city; but could not find anything that suited her, that would appeal to her emotions, that was different yet decorative.

She decided to search out-of-town galleries and left New York heading north. One day she noticed the small green grass hill in Cape

Breton on which stood a picturesque, but old and aged gray barn. Parts of it had fallen away and were strewn upon the ground. The barn seemed to be calling to her. She was fascinated and slowly walked over to investigate.

A particular flat plank of antiqued gray wood caught her attention. It was as long as her outstretched arm and as wide as her spread fingers. The edges were jagged where it had broken away from the deteriorating structure. The knots in the wood were reminiscent of the eyes of an old man, wrinkled and weary but intense with a secret knowledge of the past. There seemed to be a nose and an open mouth like the one in Munch's "The Scream." As she touched the wood the gray grain by the mouth seemed to curve into a smile as though it was enjoying the caress. It was like petting the face of someone sad and ancient, who was so tired that he did not even have the strength to shave off his white stubble.

She fell in love with this awesome wooden plank. It would look perfect on her dining-room wall. She carefully wrapped it in a blanket and tenderly put it into the trunk of her car. Not only would it add charm to the room but it would continue to evoke her loving feelings.

She was wrong! Something strange happened to her treasure when they were back in New York. The antique gray color seemed to turn a sickly, sorrowful, bitter green. The lines no longer smiled and the eyes had closed shut. It looked forlorn and ugly. She pitied the sad plank of wood; she no longer loved it, no longer needed it, and no longer wanted it. Yet she did not have the heart to throw it away. It was left leaning on a railing outside on the terrace where it continues to wither and decay.

Guilt feelings swell inside of her when she looks at her lost prize. She had torn it from its own home and taken it to a strange environment. It did not belong there. Dead leaves are gathering on the sad discarded old wooden man. She thinks he died.

Red Roses

I love rainy days
The mood outside
    reflects the sadness in me.

The dull wailing water
    beats a message
    on my window.

It is conversation to my
    Loneliness

And yet, while the blue
    Heavens cry,
And my heavy heart
    Weighs down the falling leaves,
The red roses will bloom again and again.

♦ ♦ ♦ ♦ ♦

About the Author

Marion was born and raised in the East Flatbush section of Brooklyn, New York. She attended PS 135 where she discovered her love for art and writing. Upon graduation from Tilden High School, her yearbook caption read, "Marion believes the right way is the write way."

She worked as a secretary while going to Brooklyn College (Evening School), she fell in love, got married, abandoned school and created two wonderful children who gave her three beautiful grandchildren, who gave her three (plus-one-on-the-way) delightful great- grandchildren.

During her child raising years, Marion was active in community affairs: serving as the Editor-in-Chief of the PTA newspaper, organizing a petition for new schools, protesting the war in Vietnam, and pursuing better education standards. At the young age of 43, she became a matriculated student at Queens College in New York and four years later entered the salaried work force.

She and her husband retired to West Palm Beach, Florida, where she attended college, (again) studying art. She was elected into the Palm Beach Art Guild, participated in art shows, and conducted adult art workshops for seniors. She also volunteered as a docent for The Norton Art Museum.

Marion resumed her love of writing after moving to Leisure World, Maryland.

CHAPTER 9

Artscape

By Denise Barker

The Bronx

Something about the Bronx,
is down to earth in a concrete and tar
sort of way.
From Spuyten Dyvil at the north
to Yankee Stadium further south
It's a place that knows its own.
Swanky Manhattan across the river,
doesn't faze the Bronx.
And to the west the Long Island Sound
minds its business.
people walk and work and
fish and drink and never
doubt the ground beneath their feet.

Artscape

People dancing in the street
is always a good sign.
Giant artworks on the avenue
awaken the mind.
The smell of roasting beef,
and frying dough,
The smoke rises from the grills to burn the eyes
On this corner Swahili dancers stomp
barefoot on the steaming pavement.
On the stage a salsa band is tuning up.
In tiny booths surrounded by gauzy curtains,
Artists sell shiny silver pieces;
small sculptures of frogs and turtles.
At the foot of the hill, a blues band plays
in front of the railroad station
and hundreds on the slope
feel the almost visible music
rise up in the warm damp air.

Waiting for Rain

She stands at the window, waiting for rain.
To sit at the table is too much to bear
The house is too empty, too quiet, like death.
The funeral was yesterday, she feels he's still there.

The friends have all gone now, back to their homes,
The food is moldering in the dark dining room

There are things to be done, there are forms to be
filed,
But not this day, not by her, not now.

She's seeing a man walk by on the street,
Along the forsythia path to the wood.
The jacket's the same, the lift of the head.
She leans towards the window and gasps.

He turns and his face is within her sight.
It's not really the one who is lost.
And finally the rain falls; a deluge, a flood
Of warm tears on the cold pane of her face.

Magoo: a Dog Story

We wanted a small dog, a benji, a pup
not a hulking Heinz 57 like you.

Sad, nearsighted Doberman mix,
sitting in the corner
like a chastised child.

"She shakes hands."
The woman said.
And you did, raising a black and tan paw.
And we fell madly in love
with your lop-eared face
and decidedly goofy demeanor.

You moved right in and ate a shoe,
A watch and several books;
Dozens of Christmas cookies, a loaf of beef,
All disappeared from the table.

The day you leaped into the air
And swallowed a threatening bee,
The kids proclaimed you a hero
And gave you their lunch desserts.

Claustrophobic and nervous, you leaped through windows
And hurled your sad self against heavy closed doors
And sulked for weeks about being left in the kennel.

Sad, silly, loyal, fur-faced friend.
We miss you.

Pop

My father was a hippie before there were hippies,
A pacifist when we didn't know the word.
He dreamed of tropical skies,
while he worked in the dark of the subway.

He told great stories, mostly imagined.
The one about being a tree surgeon was true.
The one about knowing Mark Twain, I don't think so.

Born in 1890, he never believed they landed on the moon.
Only schooled to 7th grade, he could recite whole scenes of Shakespeare.
He died in '70. I haven't seen him since, but I see him more clearly now.

The Stoop

Where I lived when I was little
We all had stoops;
Stone steps or benches of concrete and brick
Affixed to the front of the building.

Gritty and dusty in the summer heat,
Bleachers of the street arena
Box seats to the daily drama of the west Bronx.

Waiting for Good Humor,
Watching for friends,
Giggling over the boy
Who delivered the groceries
Listening to stories of the war and the depression
Picking the scabs from skinned knees
And peeling our sunburns.
Our days unraveled from the skeins of our lives
As our mothers knitted and chatted
Till 5:00 when the fathers came home.

About the Author

Denise grew up in New York City and lived in Colorado and Maryland. She spent many happy days working in libraries, and occasionally writing for local papers.

CHAPTER 10

My Amazing Life

By Joanie Friedlander

Gun Totin' Cowboy

"Gun Totin' Cowboy Arrested At Morris Plains Apartment Complex Last Night!"

That was the headline in next morning's paper when my cowboy playing child-husband, Tommy, fully outfitted with his Western cowboy hat, cowboy boots, vest, holster, and a gun-belt loaded with live bullets pointed his silver-plated actual Colt 45 pistol at the car that was illegally parked in our Reserved Parking Spot.

But I'm getting ahead of myself.

That evening, I had arrived home from work to find someone had parked in our parking space. I was quite upset and I parked my car in a place for Visitors. I quickly burst into our new apartment, and loudly declared, "Someone is parked in our parking space!"

To my surprise and shock, while I was out making a living for both of us, Tommy was "playing cowboy" like a child. He had the telephone receiver in his hand and he announced, "I'll take care of that...your Mother's on the phone." He handed me the phone and rushed past me out the door.

I yelled after him, "Wait Tommy, you can't go out like that!" Then I put the receiver to my ear. Mom reassured me, "He's a grown man, Joanie, he'll be alright." As I tried to explain to her how he was dressed, I heard a woman screaming from the parking lot, and then police sirens.

"Gotta go, Mom, something's happening," I told my mother, who was calling from Florida. I quickly hung up, and rushed out the door and downstairs to our parking lot.

The man was holding Tommy down; called Tommy a curse word I had never heard in my life. I yelled at the man, "He's not a mother, he's my husband!"

A woman admonished me, "How can you let your husband go out in public like that? Don't you realize there's been a double-murder in this neighborhood?"

Before I could say another word, two policemen came, they cuffed Tommy and he was taken to the local jail. I followed the cop cars to see where he was going and phoned my sister, Merrily, who is a lawyer in Virginia, because I was at a loss at what to do. Merrily called Richard, our cousin, who was a local lawyer; and Richard bailed him out so Tommy wouldn't have to stay in jail overnight.

Needless to say: we were kicked out of the apartment complex the next day.

Good Vibrations

I walked down my front steps to begin my daily walk, and made a left.

A beautiful sparrow, sitting on the metal fence looked right at me - and you were here.

I watched him, until he flew away - to the metal fence on the side of my building and you were here.

I followed him, and re-discovered that crepe myrtle tree blooming with flowers of your favorite color - and you were here.

Then our sparrow flew to a tree, I followed and saw the most fantastic garden with a baby cupid, and a young girl angel who was looking right at the bright orange flowers, the type I planted for my baby daughter when we moved into our Iowa house - and you were here.

Next that sparrow led me to a path; I took it to a bench - another sparrow seemed to invite me to sit on that bench - I did - and you were here.

Next I walked up and down upon the places that you park when you visit me or pick me up, or drop me off - and you were here.

A woman, about my age, with three different color flowers blooming upon her cool top (each with a dragonfly in front of it - dragonflies are said to bring good luck, by the way.) She and I talked until she spotted her friend and left. Was I alone, no siree! - you are here - right here with me and together we're on top of the world.

Yippee and Wahoo, Oh Yeah, do I ever love you!!!

(. . . and here in my heart you will stay, forever and a day . . .)

No, Not The End - Just Our Beginning.

Awkward First Dates

In high school I belonged to an after-school group. One day, I invited the whole group over to my home for a party. I figured they were nice people to have as friends.

Everyone seemed to be having a good time, listening to music and dancing.

All of a sudden, one guy, who I didn't even know his name - out of the blue - declared his "undying love" for me and announced, "When we are married, you need to keep a Kosher home!"

I am Jewish, but we didn't grow up in a Kosher home, and I didn't even know this fellow from Adam! What prompted him to tell me he was going to marry me!? I did not give him any hints that I was even interested in him.

Even though I told him, "No!" He kept following me and pestering me.

Good thing my cousin, Andrew was in the other room with my mom - I told Andrew to please throw this fellow out of my house - and he did. Thank goodness.

Technically, that wasn't even a date (smile.)

I never saw the silly fella again - I didn't go back to that after-school group.

(When my family moved to New Jersey from Chicago, I was eight years old and Andrew was seven. I had a childhood crush on him.)

Recently, I mentioned to Andrew that when I first met him as a child, I had a puppy love crush on him. To my surprise, he confessed he had a crush on me (when he was a child also!)

Thank goodness for friendly relatives.

Then in college, a really handsome, and nice fellow asked me to his frat party. As I lived walking distance from his dorm, I told him that I would meet him there.

This was to be our first date ... or so I believed (was I simply naïve?)

When I arrived, I looked around for him, and there he was, on a couch, heavily making out with another girl. He looked up at me, and said, "Hi Joelle." (I chose to go back to using my birth name in college.)

Surprised, but taking it all in stride; I turned around and walked back home.

Thankfully, I never saw him again.

About a decade after my divorce, I went with my Red Hat Society sister to one of those speed-dating events where you meet tons of guys for only four minutes at a time.

I was very impressed with one guy who used his four minutes to sing "Schubert" for me. When he mentioned he was in a choir that sang the music of classical musicians, such as Schubert, I asked him if he could please, use his minutes to sing just to me. Was I ever thrilled!

As it turned out, we both had chosen each other. Finally, the day came for me to have my first date with him.

I asked him to please meet me at the Starbucks across the street from my apartment, and he did.

We went to a nice Italian restaurant (that I picked out.) It was just a few doors down from the Starbucks.

The entire time, he talked about how upset he was that his mother threw out all his baseball cards. I found him quite interesting and I think I did see it from his point of view.

After lunch, he walked me back to Starbucks and said, "I can tell that you like me more than I like you. Sorry, but I won't be calling you." (Oh, no! Not again!?)

Oh well, you win some; you lose some. I told him it was alright so, once again, I back walked home alone.

About a month later, he did call me, but only to tell me that he now was in a financial business for himself, and if either I invested money with him, or I found someone to do it, he would treat me to another lunch.

(No way, Jose!) I said, "No, thank you," and I never heard from him again.

To end on a happy note, my current boyfriend now is better than all the rest!

Innocence Lost and Found

I was 21 years old living away from my New Jersey home, on my own, for the very first time, a junior in college in Brooklyn, New York. The most my high school boyfriend and I ever did was kiss with our lips with our clothes on.

At Pratt Institute, I had a crush on my new friend, a senior. It never occurred to me, not to trust him, so I eagerly went to his apartment when he invited me there. To my surprise and shock, he pulled off my clothes, and started kissing me on my neck. Having grown up watching those horror films, I truly thought he was a vampire, drinking my blood. I screamed, "Don't! Stop! Stop!" but now he was raping me, much to my virgin horror and shame. I was in so much pain, both physically and emotionally.

Somehow, I got back to my brownstone where I lived off campus. I remember simply sitting on the floor in front of one of my paintings, staring at the painted blue sky. The next thing I recall was Mom and Merrily, my sister, standing at the foot of the hospital bed, talking to each other, "She went into it fast, so she should be coming out of it fast, too."

I found out much later I was not talking, not responding, just sitting in my brownstone room; and my roommate called my mom. Mom came to take me home, I was black and blue from bruises to my face and body and I was "catatonic." Mom took me to the Carrier Clinic in New York where I was admitted and given shock treatments.

I remember I had to relearn how to talk, walk, and Merrily had to teach me about sex.

About a year later after Merrily moved out, Mom and Michael, my brother, were planning to move to Florida from New Jersey. I took a temporary job until our house was sold. That's where I met Tommy. Believing I had only "half-a-brain" remaining, I immediately accepted when Tommy asked me to marry him after only two weeks of knowing each other.

Common sense eventually returned when I got a divorce with the freedom to live my own life!

My precious daughter, Jill was the best thing that came from the marriage. Now, I'm the proud grandma of Malachi, Ava, and Devon. Another grandchild, Arielle, is our little angel in Heaven watching over us. She passed at 19 days old from complications of being premature.

I now feel truly blessed.

After My Divorce

My Man, you're my sunshine; so bright - my rainbow: Right!
Whenever I need you, you're here; bringing me good sense, and
   love, and cheer (you bring me perspective.)
You always see the glass half-full and encourage me to also be still
   inside.
You're my sunshine after the storm.
Your loving words and examples in your own life keep me strong.
"When we least expect it, people step up to help us along."
You are mine, and I am thine (you taught me how to love again.)
Oh Yes! I am forever grateful to you and to God for bringing us
   together.
Because our love is true - we help each other through the good and
   the bad in all kinds of weather.
Sometimes we take a walk down memory lane, sometimes we make
   new memories again and again.
In happy times and other, we'll stay together through it all to help

each other; and learn from each other while discovering more about ourselves.

To have and to hold from then and now as we grow older, not old because we will always stay young at heart.

We live in the reality of the light and raindrops and rainbows.

We are high on the joy of being alive and sharing God's gifts of the earth and the sky and the birds, flying high.

You are my sunshine. You are my rainbow.

And I love you very much.

May everyone find the happiness we share together.

And be as blessed as we are.

About the Author

Joanie was born into a family filled with art and music. Her Dad played classical violin while her Mom accompanied him on their console piano. She spent her free hours writing poetry, stories, and doing art (sketching and painting).

Joanie also enjoys playing the piano and guitar. She loved playing the viola in her High School orchestra, as well as the Glockenspiel in the marching band.

When Joanie and her only child, Jill, were going through a hurtful divorce, she wrote and illustrated a children's book. Joanie let Jill rewrite Joanie's original story in Jill's own flowery language. Joanie and Jill went house-to-house selling copies as coloring books. Joanie still sketches and enjoys watercolor painting for fun and gifts.

Currently, Joanie enjoys sharing her writings with her new friends in the Writers Group.

CHAPTER 11

David

By Viola Stendardi

David was only six or seven years old when his bubbling imagination and artistic ability began to take shape. At the time, his father worked in a printing house in lower Manhattan, and almost always came home with whatever unused paper and paper products he could find. Better in his hands than the trash because he could bring it all home to David, snatches and scraps, leftovers of plain bond paper, colored construction paper, oak tag, cardboard, etc., all stuffed into a large envelope. David couldn't wait to see what the day's envelope contained.

The material became the cornerstone of a wonderful gift. David painted, cut out, pasted together to create all sorts of things: posters, paintings, cut-out figurines, buildings, and most notably, his castles.

It was difficult for me to understand why I couldn't do the same.

David would say, "You can do it. Just try." But of course I could not. He and I were cousins, and although five years older, I could not create anything artistic or useful. No matter what.

He shared everything he made. "Here, take this home," he would say, indicating some choice article and stuffing it into a shopping bag, together with all sorts of other things, including the paper dolls he had designed especially for me and his ubiquitous castles.

Early in our childhood, he was astute enough to catch on to my lack of siblings, and asserted, "You know, I'm not your cousin. I'm your brother."

David understood the need I have felt most of my life - perhaps better than I - and became the brother I lacked - a wonderful, loving, caring man who never ceased to be a strong positive influence in my life. From time to time, he would remind me, "Remember, you're my sister."

I feel I can safely say that in the ultimate sense of the word, he was everyone's brother. He would help anyone and everyone - unselfishly, unstintingly, untiringly - friends, relatives, the elderly, and colleagues. He was always willing to share his knowledge and experience. Especially, young musicians whom he introduced to the likes of Purcell, Handel, Dowland, Giordano, and Scarlotti to expose them to the relationship between music and words. David loved music, words, and language. He passed his love on to the rest of us.

David became an art teacher and art historian. Throughout his life, he took pleasure in the visual and graphic arts, and possessed a love for natural beauty with an astute eye for what was pleasing and attractive. He was an excellent teacher, but the essence of what was important to him went well beyond teaching. It rested, I believe, in his sensitivity for people and his generous spirit of friendship. Anyone who desired to be his friend became his friend. David shared whatever he possessed with the world: his extraordinary artistic talent; unique knowledge of the art, art history and music worlds; his quickness to welcome and assist, and the ability to so freely lend himself to the needs of others.

An incident of his caring, recounted to me many years ago by one colleague, involved a student David had found sitting in the corner of a hallway floor at school, ear plugs in place, obliviously listening to music. The student was a Down Syndrome child. David leaned over to ask what she was listening to, and she happily replied, "The music for The Nutcracker." Thereon began a wonderful friendship. David negotiated with the Special Education department, the Board of Education, and the child's family for permission to take her with two of her friends, to a performance of The Nutcracker at New York City Center. Afterwards, he frequently taped and sent her music. They had many conversations over the years about music and the ballet.

Another story I recall concerned a dog left alone in a backyard for long periods of time while the owners were at work. David spoke to the individuals and arranged for a friend to take the dog. The friend and his dog were together for over 15 years, until separated by the dog's death, during all of the time he was happily well-cared for and loved.

Another experience concerned a neighbor who lost her nightly ride to the subway stop to catch her train to Manhattan where she worked cleaning offices at night. David heard of her dilemma and drove her there himself, each evening for many months, until a substitute could be located.

These were the common, ordinary circumstances calling for a kind deed, to which David's typical response was to intervene whenever a need existed. The 25 years he spent teaching and creating spilled over with absolute examples reaching far and wide into an array of personal and professional situations. He made it his habit to meet a problem head-on, did not believe in delaying a solution, and was never turned off by complications warranting more work on his behalf.

It was then, into the late 1980s, that a plague erupted from the very depths of the unknown. The killer AIDS was loose, and this brother to all became an early victim.

The English poet Shelly wrote these lines in a poem about someone close to him, and I recite:

> "He is a portion of the loveliness
> Which once he made more lovely."

♦ ♦ ♦ ♦ ♦

About the Author

Viola received a Bachelor of Arts from the English State University of New York. During her professional career, she was employed for 25 years as a Secretary and Office Manager for a New York City law firm.

She has completed several courses in Creative Writing at New York University and has been awarded Certificates of Recognition by Essex County, New Jersey, in the Legacies Writing Contest for 2013 and 2016.

She has also completed courses in Memoir Writing, most current instructor Lisa Romeo, teacher in a graduate MFA program and author of "Starting with Goodbye", a novel recently published by University of Nevada Press.

CHAPTER 12

Memoir Essays

By Verna Denny

75 Steps

My daughter, Janine, was thrilled about our upcoming biannual visit to Barcelona and we were looking forward to it too. Every few days she would Skype or email. "There is a cabaret performance my friend Jen is performing on Saturday night, I think it will be fun to go. Mom, I told my hula hoop teacher you were the best spinner in the housing projects. Come with me to class. I know you can still do it. I also found the best restaurant. I can't afford it, but we can go together. It's on my list."

Invariably she would end the conversation with a plea, "I wish you were staying near me instead of that hotel on the outskirts of the city." And I always firmly replied, "It will be fine. It's a Sheraton. We'll know what to expect: the sleep comfort bed, the bath mat, and the handrails. We can keep up with the presidential race with USA Today. And the room is free. We can stay there with our Starwood points."

In actuality, I was bending the facts a little bit. The unvarnished truth was I had become a Starwood point junkie. I joined the Starwood program because Janine was living abroad, specifically so that I could use the points to visit her. I calculated that if I used my Starwood credit card for absolutely everything I did in my daily life over two years I could accumulate enough points, 120,000, to stay at the first class Le Meredian, around the corner from Janine's house for 10 nights.

But on other trips I discovered the value of these points: A five-day beach stay at the Westin Fort. Lauderdale (40,000 points); an overnight stay at the Bar Harbor Maine airport (2,500 points) when we missed the last ferry to Islesford; sipping strawberry daiquiris while watching the sunset sink into the horizon (200 points); a night at the Washington DC W Hotel (12,000 points) so we could go to the theater without coming home on the Metro late at night. My point account was slowly depleting. So, when I read there was a new two-star hotel a tram ride away from Janine, and that it accepted my points (30,000 points for the same ten day stay) I jumped at the opportunity.

A few weeks before we were due to leave I got a particularly excited call from Janine, "Mom, guess what? My friend Chris is traveling for work. He's going to Uganda for two weeks and says you are welcome to stay at his apartment. No, he's not charging you anything. We can think of a gift to bring him from the States. He lives right across the plaza from me. It will be so much better than that hotel. The only thing, it's a four-floor walk up. That won't be hard for you and Dad, right?"

Another 30,000 points saved went flashing through my head as I convinced myself my quick "No problem" was due to filial devotion. I pictured wide marble steps, solid brass banisters, and one-level flights, very manageable in my mind.

The taxi from the airport left us off in front of what appeared to be a comparatively modern building with a wood and glass door with chrome handles. We stepped over the threshold into a small lobby. There was the wide staircase as I pictured and even an elevator.

"Look", I pointed happily.

"We go this way," Janine said as she led us through a tiny walkway leading to the back of the building. The open concrete courtyard floor was cracked and bulging. Bicycles and shopping carts were chained to a metal fence. Laundry lines crisscrossed the opening in the courtyard. Colorful shirts and skirts flapped in the warm breeze. Janine walked ahead of us around another corner through a tight doorway. Heading upward at a straight angle was a narrow row of stairs no wider than 12 to 18 inches, each tread about 9 inches deep. The steps were corrugated metal; the railing a filigree ironwork. If you've ever been to the Statue of Liberty and tried to negotiate the last winding staircase to the head and crown, you'll have a sense of what I mean.

"The apartment is at the top," Janine hoisted up the smaller suitcase and began the ascent. "This actually is prime real estate for this building. The apartments in the front do not have any outdoor space. Chris' apartment has a rooftop terrace as big as the apartment itself. You'll love it. You'll see."

I looked over at Harry to see how he was processing all of this, but he was already hoisting our suitcase and trying to geometrically calculate how he could maneuver it up the steps.

I grasped the handrail tentatively. It moved a bit. I pushed it harder. It was detached in places but seemed to have enough connections to hold. I held the banister on my right side and propped my left elbow against the wall on the left side and made my way up the staircase that way using the bump, bump, bump of Harry dragging the suitcase as my meditative focal point to harness my concentration. Once I made the mistake of glancing over my right shoulder and seeing the wide expanse of open space straight below to the first floor. I averted my eyes before vertigo took hold.

When I got to the top landing Janine had already entered the apartment. There was barely enough space outside the apartment door for Harry and me and the suitcase.

"I can't do this," I said.

"Yes you can," Harry replied.

(Later I would sneak off and call all the hotels in Barcelona however because of a soccer match final there were no rooms available for points or money.)

I would like to say I got more comfortable, more adept at climbing the stairs. I didn't. I did get better at counting. 75 steps times 4 trips up and down a day times 10 days equals 3,000 steps before the plane ride home.

I snuggled in that night next to my 72-year-old husband, who last year had undergone two hip replacement surgeries and now carried a suitcase up 75 steps. He put his arm around me as he relaxed into the mattress and let out an extended breath. "It's nice being considered healthy and young and capable," he sighed. "It's nice being seen through Janine's eyes."

Hope and Honor on Mother's Day

No one had anything bad to say about Ruthie's on Yelp. To be exact, one person did have a ho-hum remark, in sharp contrast to rave reviews of the mac and cheese (smooth and creamy), the Arnold Palmer (so sweet but isn't that the way it's supposed to be?), and the collard greens (the best I've ever tasted). But there's always one dissenter. (What does someone named Clarisse know about anything anyway?)

So that's how I ended up on Mother's Day at Ruthie's, the premiere soul food take-out in all of Brooklyn which happened to be right down the block.

I've been staying at my friend's empty apartment (who as luck would have it is traveling) located near the doctor, while my husband is recovering from hip surgery. Being the primary caregiver invokes mega mom tasks (even though I'm not Harry's mom) like emptying the urine bottles and putting on socks. So, I've been feeling overburdened and very momish in a way I hadn't felt since my youngest went off to college eight years ago.

That must be why it was so easy for me to slip, once again, into a self-sacrificing stance so often satirized as a basic mom trait, when I suggested, and even felt proud of, the idea of going out for my Mother's Day dinner the Friday before, at a local Mexican restaurant for the luncheon special where for ten dollars you could get a soup or salad, a house mojito, and a huge platter of mole chicken with rice and beans. How thoughtful and thrifty.

Now, on Mother's Day, I'm feeling a little bit down and out and there is this empty space that needs to be filled. I know from past years I won't get a call from my daughter who lives in Barcelona. (They don't celebrate Mother's Day there so no memory cues.) My daughter, who is in California, may call but with the four-hour time difference coast to coast it may not come until late at night (and Dad recuperating probably didn't make the reminder call). It's too late to join the church ladies in their fuchsia lace dresses and white straw hats for Mother's Day brunch at the downtown Marriott.

Oh, what I would give for one of those overpriced bouquets of carnations every gal and guy on the street seems to be carrying to their moms. Ruthie's is my last-ditch effort to rescue the day.

As an aside, I have been enjoying this visit to Fort Greene. Harry's doctor assigned an exercise routine requiring him to do incrementally longer walks each day, so we've had a chance to explore this gentrifying neighborhood, providing a nice mixture of nostalgia and immersion in what's vibrant and current. Stately renovated row houses abut sidewalks that are cracked and bulging from neglect or from the roots of aged oak trees. Liquor stores with their gated plastic safety windows still stand among trendy boutiques. Parents, pushing Bugaboo strollers, brush past the upturned hands of beggars.

There is a long line at Ruthie's but it's not an impatient line. The group is soothed by the crisp, sharp smell of fried chicken that coats the room in promises to come. The women waiting are dressed in hats and flowered prints with patent leather shoes. There are only two seats for them at a plastic kitchen table pushed against the wall. The rest lean or sway. The men are more casually dressed in African-style shirts.

A young Asian man enters, his eyes flickering uncomfortably across the room. "It's my first time here," he says to no one in particular. One of the women takes his elbow in her gloved hand. "This is the window to order. We're just waiting. Now be sure to get the fried chicken or whiting if you prefer."

"The caramel apple pie too," another adds.

I feel a rush of satisfaction, and my mouth waters in anticipation, knowing the order I placed matches these recommendations.

Others come and go. A row of cars stands outside, engines running. Cars doors open as customers come out with long plastic bags stacked with round to-go boxes, balancing quart sized Styrofoam containers of lemonade and sweet tea they hand over before driving away. I enjoy watching the going-ons.

Into this mix arrives a young mother. She appears no older than eighteen. Her two daughters, ages two and three, stand shyly behind. The girl settles into the line, glancing and nodding. She is wearing a short-patterned skirt and a nylon blouse. Her hair is lengthened by an inexpensive weave, noticeably crooked on her head. The little girls stand politely at their mother's side, barely squirming, dressed in black taffeta dresses with deep gray netting and pink ribbon trim, their legs lotioned and shiny.

I'm probably not the only one thinking about how different this scenario is from others we've seen: the teen mother, provocatively dressed, gabbing on the cell phone, yelling at her children to be quiet, and then threatening to slap them.

As the line moves and the young mother gets closer to the window one of the women approaches her. "Are you buying your own dinner?" she asks. The girl nods. The woman opens her satin, pleated purse, her wide brimmed yellow hat dipping as she searches inside and pulls out a twenty-dollar bill. She crushes it into the girl's palm. "Happy Mother's Day."

And I smile - we all smile - and suddenly everything is very right with the world.

About the Author

Writing has been an integral part of Verna's life as long as she can remember - and she has a drawer of rejection letters to prove it. A poem from her dark stage was published in her junior high school magazine ("Hope was reborn for this she knew. Though death holds the door life must walk through.") followed by a plethora of writing during her high school years. Volumes of diaries and journals she kept were deemed too steamy and tossed before taking marriage vows. She wishes she had them now.

Verna minored in creative writing in college and took many courses during the years as she honed her skills and just had fun with words. But it wasn't until she joined the Writers Group of Leisure World, attending her first meeting while the movers were unpacking, that she developed a regular writing practice. Knowing she would need something new and fresh to share at the next meeting and being part of a group of dedicated writers was inspirational. Over the past eight years, with the support and encouragement of other writers, she has written a collection of memoir essays and is working on her first novel.

CHAPTER 13

Deer Tales

By Woody Shields

The white-tailed deer is a beautiful animal. The endearing features and slender body have captured the affection of millions. Only the most vile of humans could gaze into the soft lovable large brown eyes and experience contempt for one of nature's greatest creatures.

White-tailed deer are many things to many people, both real and imagined, evoking a perception as unique as each of our personalities. Each perception viewed from the eyes of the beholder is influenced by our prior knowledge and experience. Through fleeting encounters, our human nature transforms perception into reality.

White-tailed deer are many things to many people, accommodating each of our personal perceptions. Similar to our other choices in life, challenges exist to understand the perceptions of others with a different set of knowledge and experience, and to understand the foundation of their perceptions (and others to understand ours). The perception (theirs or ours) is neither for the better nor worse, rather different.

Gullible Hunter

By human nature, we are vulnerable to a constant barrage of fads and gimmicks to improve our quality of life. Our storage closets are full of trinkets. Likewise, a deer hunter is also receptive to any innovation to improve the quest to gain an advantage over the competition. He is easy prey for the scam artists who push the limits of credibility to separate the gullible hunter from his money. The buyer must beware.

Every successful American sport is exploited by commercialization, deer hunting is no exception. The enormous purchasing power of the hunter supports the development of thousands of new deer hunting products, magazines, books, and videos claiming to unravel the secrets of deer behavior, the magic tidbit of information to make a difference.

Years ago, the principle reward for a master hunter was the respect of peers, a few became local legends. The master hunter would normally only share his secrets with a small circle of companions. Secrecy was necessary to protect his advantage over other hunters. The sharing of information with strangers was not beneficial.

Commercialization changed the definition of the hunting legend. Today, the legends of the sport are measured by the number of record book entries and product endorsements, an unfortunate shift in the rich heritage of the sport.

The vast majority of commercial hunters are honest folk, who do obey hunting laws and believe the products they endorse, although a few are not. The latter few are the poachers who engage in illegal activities to kill large antlered bucks to maintain their status as a hunting legend and their primary source of income. Others include the scam artists who will do or say anything to make a dollar.

Regardless of the claims of the scam artists, deer hunting is hard work. The most difficult challenge is sighting a deer within the effective range of weaponry, a tribute to the advanced survival skills of the white-tailed deer. Any product which claims to improve the number of deer sightings is an instant success. The products generally claim to defeat (or exploit) the deer's keen senses of sight, hearing, and smell.

Deer are particularly wary of their surroundings and the detection of a hunter will likely trigger an instinct to evade the potential threat. Camouflage patterns on outer clothing are designed to blend with the surroundings to conceal a hunter's presence. Among the other products to minimize detection are Ultra-Violent (UV) light neutralizers, scent free soaps, non-scented detergents, scent eliminators, scent absorbing clothing, and cover scents (such as raccoon, red fox, or skunk) to mask the human odor.

The challenge is accepting the outrageous claims of the product's effectiveness. One moment the salesman describes the white-tailed deer as an elusive creature of the forest. The next moment, he claims his product will transform the brilliant animal into a vulnerable creature of habit.

Attractants containing deer urine generate the most controversy. Huge profit margins have enticed thousands of vendors to the market, both national and local. The ingredients in a small bottle of deer urine, priced between ten and forty dollars, costs a few dollars to manufacture.

Unfortunately, the quality of the product is not controlled by any regulatory agency, except the marketplace. Although the vast majority of products contain actual deer urine, the urine of other ungulate mammals (such as sheep and cows) may be substituted. The battle for market share is brutal with each vendor claiming others cut (or water down) their urine products.

The doe-in-heat urine products are especially popular with a gullible hunter. The products claim to contain doe urine collected during the estrus period. The theory suggests a mature buck is attracted and driven nearly crazy by the odor of a doe in heat. Accordingly, a mature buck while preoccupied with estrus scent will be vulnerable to a hunter.

The contents of doe-in-heat urine products are highly questionable. A number of scent manufacturers claim their products contain the active component of estrus urine. The products also claim to contain a secret mixture of preservatives and stabilizers to extend the shelf life of the product.

The active component of doe-in-heat urine is the chemical structure known as a pheromone, an extremely volatile compound. By nature's design, pheromones must be short lived to prevent the buck tending the doe for an extended time. Also, pheromones are extremely difficult to collect and to detect even in the best medical laboratories. Furthermore, the deer biologists are currently unable to determine exactly when the doe enters the 24 hour estrus period.

Another observation, humans also produce pheromones. If the technology exists to collect and bottle pheromones, why doesn't anyone collect and bottle human pheromones, a more profitable business than selling deer urine?

The bottom line on deer urine products (contrary to what a deer urine salesman says), a deer's response (if any) to urine products is not completely understood. Any response is more likely related to the deer's curiosity than to sexual attraction.

Is Deer Hunting Really Better than Sex?

During the intense moments before the shot, every hunter will usually claim he was in complete command of his emotions. He is lying, unless he is a killing machine. A typical hunter experiences an adrenalin surge, appropriately called *buck fever*.

The reaction is inherited from the primitive instinct of our human ancestors. Stimulation of the adrenal glands injects adrenalin into the blood stream to prepare the body for action, a survival mechanism. As described by medical specialists, the adrenal response may occur when one of five stimuli (the five f's) is present: fear, fight, fright, mating, and buck fever.

Whatever the definition, buck fever (mild or severe) is the normal reaction for most hunters. The symptoms are generally mild, such as moderate increases in heart rate, blood pressure, and respiration rate. A high level of adrenalin may make the heart thump causing every artery to pulsate, weakening in the arms and legs, and pounding in the temples.

Buck fever contributes to the thrill of the hunt with memorable moments for a lifetime. Deer hunting is often described as hours of boredom interspersed with moments of sheer terror. However brief, the moments may be extremely intense. The intensity of symptoms varies from mild excitement to a psychological orgasm to total impairment. Deer hunting can really be better than sex.

A number of hunters reserve the term *buck fever* to describe the condition of total impairment accompanied by bizarre, almost humorous symptoms, such as uncontrollable shaking, ejecting a full magazine of cartridges without firing a shot, or yelling "Bang" each time the trigger is pulled with an empty firearm. Other hunters are so immobilized the simple act of aiming is impossible. A few hunters become paralyzed and may even faint at the sight of a deer.

For an individual hunter, the reaction to a given situation depends on prior experience. A hunter will normally feel comfortable if he has previously encountered a similar event, like staring down a large antlered buck standing at twenty feet. Less experienced hunters are susceptible to more intense symptoms.

The amount of time available for adrenalin to impact the hunter's actions is related to the intensity of the symptoms. A hunter may not have sufficient time to get excited when a deer magically appears, the ideal situation. As the time lengthens between the initial sighting and the shot, the amount of adrenalin increases. The choice of weaponry is also a factor. Bowhunters must generally wait longer for an acceptable shot than firearm hunters, permitting higher levels of adrenalin.

Buck fever is responsible for a greater number of missed shots than poor marksmanship. Disbelief and incoherent mumbling are common reactions. The memory of a missed opportunity may haunt a hunter for a lifetime.

A special form of buck fever can occur when shooting at a large antlered buck. The hunter may miss when the deer is so close he can describe the detailed structure of the antlers. When a hunter is distracted with antlers, the buck could not be safer. To make a successful shot, the hunter must concentrate on the body, not the antlers. There will be plenty of time for counting points when the shooting is done. A master hunter always focuses attention on a spot on the deer's body, the point of aim.

Buck fever may also occur after the shot, either as a euphoric high or a devastating despair after an unexplainable miss. Upon shooting a deer, a hunter may vocalize his emotions with a shout of joy, such as "Yahoo." Another hunter may enter a state of shock, unable to field dress his deer or to find his way out of the woods.

After shooting a deer, a hunter may be unable to perform simple tasks. The hunter may need to return to the harvest site to retrieve any forgotten items, including his rifle, bow, treestand, backpack, knife, hat, cell phone, etc.

The time a hunter may be susceptible to adrenalin-induced behavior is not limited to the act of hunting. For avid hunters, the anticipation of the hunt may be sufficient to release low levels of adrenalin for several days before a major event, such as the opening day of firearms season. An elevated level of adrenalin may cause a noticeable change in a hunter's sleep patterns, a general feeling of restlessness. He may have difficulty falling asleep and may wake up early. An adrenalin-induced sleepless night before the hunt is normal for less experienced hunters.

Another interesting aspect of the adrenal response is the experience called time capture where the brain functions as a slow motion recorder. A hunter's world pauses as time stands still. The deer halts in midstep and the arrow freezes in flight. A hunter's brain flawlessly records the thousands of images during the brief moments to be replayed countless times during his lifetime. Amazingly, the same brain cannot recall the date of a wedding anniversary or a birthday.

Hunter-Employer Relationships

In today's competitive environment, retaining a stable workforce is a continuing challenge for employers. Changing jobs every few years is the norm. Every employer knows certain employees are worth more than others. Avid deer hunters are outstanding employees, more productive than their coworkers.

An avid hunter is willing to commit to a difficult task for a lifetime, such as a lengthy employment career. He works a full day's work for a full day's pay, a positive work ethic. The active lifestyle of an avid hunter results in fewer sick days and higher productivity.

An employer who accommodates the scheduling demands of deer season can retain a stable and productive workforce. Nevertheless, the proper balance between full-time employment and deer hunting presents unique challenges for both the employer and the hunter. Understanding the behavior of an avid hunter is essential for the employer to achieve a productive relationship with the hunter. Likewise, the hunter needs to understand the needs of the employer to maintain production to pay the employee's wages, a mutual benefit for both parties.

An avid hunter divides his available time, a precious commodity, between his professional, family, and hunting lives. Over the year, his professional and family lives demand the largest share of his time, about equally divided between family and job commitments. However, deer season results in a temporary, although dramatic, shift in time allocation from his usual family and job priorities.

An employer may strengthen company loyalty by accommodating the temporary shift in priorities, knowing the hunter will return to his professional life with a renewed dedication. The accommodation spreads goodwill throughout the year.

Vacation flexibility is a major concern for an avid hunter. A hunter is attracted to an employer with flexible vacation rules. Although the general timing of deer seasons are normally known in advance, a number of state wildlife agencies do not finalize the exact dates until spring, sometimes as late as June. If an employer requires the hunter to schedule vacation dates at the beginning of the year, an unexpected change in dates may result in a conflict. Scheduling difficulties are compounded for a multi-state hunter.

Deer hunters prefer to hunt first days when deer activity and the success rates are higher than other days. Harvest statistics reveal the first day of firearms season is the single best day for hunter success, about 25 percent of the annual deer harvest normally occurs on the first day of firearms season. Other important first days may include the first day of archery season, first day of muzzleloader season, first day of antlerless season, and first Saturday of firearms season.

Hunting on first days provides a substantial psychological advantage to offset the small number of expected deer sightings. With the best of conditions on the first day, the average hunter can only expect to see about half a dozen deer. Deer sightings are even fewer on other days.

In other words, all hunters expect to hunt the first day which can cause a scheduling challenge for employers. Other days are not the same. Every deer harvested on the first day is one less deer available to harvest on following days.

Over the years, employers have discovered a variety of successful strategies to accommodate their deer hunters. A number of employers, including a number of state governments and school systems, declare a holiday for the first day of firearms season. When both the employer and the employee are hunters, there is a perfect fit. Another proven strategy may include moving the work day to the prior Sunday (if the first day falls on Monday) and permitting flexible work hours during deer season to accommodate half-day hunts, or to follow a blood trail the next morning.

Another strategy empowers the hunters in the business to develop a fair vacation policy for deer season. The policy should retain flexibility for last minute changes. A hunter, who filled his tag during bow season, may voluntarily swap vacation days to allow another to hunt the first day of firearms season.

Difficult choices must be made when the company must remain open and the workforce of non-hunters is insufficient to cover the workload. The work policy must be fair and consistent. If the hunter cannot be accommodated, a higher rate of absenteeism may be expected during deer season.

An avid hunter, who is denied the opportunity to hunt the first day, is at high risk for sudden illness. The wife is often tasked to deliver the bad news to the employer. The ailment, lasting about one day, may be highly contagious.

Upon the hunter's return to work, an employer should spend a few minutes to inquire about the results of the hunt. The sincere interest of his supervisor shows concern about an important event in a hunter's life, similar to the birth of a child or the health of a family member.

Deer Camp Experience

As a hunter proceeds through his hunting career, membership in a deer camp is recommended for the complete hunting experience. Deer camp provides each of the essential elements identified in a study by the U.S. Fish and Wildlife Service on how deer hunters derive their enjoyment from deer hunting, such as escapism, nature, adventure, companionship, tradition, challenge, and accomplishment.

Deer camp provides the hunter with the opportunity to get away from it all to experience the great outdoors, a challenge to survive in the wilderness like his forefathers. Every day at deer camp is special, not to be repeated. Deer camp connects a hunter with the larger family of deer hunters, a shared sense of belonging.

Deer camp also provides acceptance where success in shooting a deer is the exception rather than the rule. The competition to shoot the first or the biggest deer in camp becomes a contest of excuses, and a pledge to wait until next year.

Money is not a disqualifying factor. Deer camp may consist of a custom cabin, a canvas tent, the back of a pickup truck, a small shanty, or an old trailer. Any overnight shelter is acceptable, comfort is not a requirement.

A permanent camp is preferred to instill an obligation to return, an annual reunion to renew bonds between family and friends. A number of camps are passed from father to son to grandson.

The traditions of deer camp are often misunderstood by outsiders, the rules are different there. The camp traditions regulate the bounds of acceptable behavior. Frequent changes are possible. The procedure to establish new traditions is not well defined, any event occurring more than once may become a camp tradition.

Standard deer camp traditions include:

Story telling - is an art form in deer camp, a place to relive past hunts and misadventures. The old buck becomes smarter, bigger, and harder to drag with each passing year. The challenging shot (which cleanly missed) becomes an impossible shot upon reassessment. Past harvest successes are memories to be cherished and revisited each year.

Camp food - the camp motto is, 'A hungry man will eat anything.' Camp food is rarely the subject of criticism. Cooking frequently rotates between camp members. The standard camp menu of burnt potatoes and wild game is usually edible, although a number of camp members survive on a high protein diet of peanut butter and jelly sandwiches.

Personal hygiene - in most camps, indoor plumbing does not exist; outhouses are the norm. Deer camp is not a pleasant place to visit.

Card games - are a favorite tradition at many deer camps. The game of poker allows a hunter to perfect the essential skills of camouflage and deception prior to matching wits with the white-tailed deer. A late night game of poker often replaces an adrenalin-induced sleepless night prior to the hunt.

Historically, a game of poker measures a man's character, the ability to control one's emotions while looking another in the eye. Deception is crucial for success. Although the capacity for deception can diminish from inactivity, the ability can be fully restored after a couple hours of practice.

Alcohol - firearms and alcohol do not mix, although a post-hunt drink to celebrate the blessings of the hunt is acceptable.

New members - An invitation to deer camp is the highest honor a hunter can extend. New members must earn their membership in deer camp. Cooking and splitting wood are common requirements.

The acceptance of women in deer camp provides a dilemma. While the moderating influence of females is beneficial, few camps allow the practice. In general, the presence of women do not contribute to the quality of the male-bonding experience. Nevertheless, a wife is often invited to prepare the camp for the upcoming season. Overnight stays may even be authorized.

Shirt tails - to shoot at a deer and miss is an unforgivable sin. Thus an effective treatment exists to prevent another occurrence; the hunter's shirt tail is cut off to excise the shooting demons. Different camps use different procedures. While a number of camps only threaten to cut off a hunter's shirt tail, often a hunter's shirt tail is the price to pay for a mistake in judgment. One camp may use scissors to remove a small strip of the shirt. Another camp slices off the entire back of the shirt with a butcher knife. A large quantity of material is preferred to ensure the shooting demons are completely exorcised from the hunter. Too much is better than too little. Multiple misses require the sacrifice of multiple shirts. The ceremony is attended by all camp members and documented with photographs. The other camp members offer encouragement as the senior member performs the surgery. The shirt tails are accumulated and prominently displayed at camp to ward off future misses.

About the Author

Woody is an avid deer hunter and a writer. His technical education is as a Navy nuclear engineer. During 37 years of Naval service, he served in challenging leadership positions where he authored tens of thousands of documents with meticulous precision, every word carefully chosen to convey a precise meaning. As writing bears the author's soul, technical writing can never be great. In his new journey, Woody bears the heart and soul of his hunting companions, forbidden areas even to the women they love.

With over 50 years of hunting with family and friends, he captures the love for the joys of life, family struggles, successes, failures, and the life experiences of a hunter. Although he has never been shy on sharing his own experiences, he finds attentive listening to the thoughts and feelings of his fellow hunters to be the most enlightening.

CHAPTER 14

Life in DC

By Anne Doherty Rinn

What It Means to be a Washingtonian

My daughter spent some time with a volunteer group called "Amigos" in the Dominican Republic. One day on the beach she was asked where she was from. "Washington, DC," she replied. They asked her, "What part of New York is that?" Imagine, someone not knowing where this beautiful city is.

As my parents were Irish immigrants I think it meant a lot to them to live and raise their children in Washington, DC, the Capitol of the United States. Every year they took us to the White House, the Tidal Basin, or the Monument grounds for Easter egg rolling. When I was fourteen we were allowed to get a workers permit. The teenagers knew the downtown district quite well since we worked at the department stores located close to Pennsylvania Avenue and the White House. We could go anywhere on the good and affordable transportation system. Our father had a pass which allowed us to travel free on Sundays which usually meant going to Glen Echo Park.

LIFE IN DC

Surprisingly, my Irish father got me out of bed early one morning to see the young Princess Elizabeth pass by Lincoln Road near our home. She raised her hand in a wave at the window; she was so small. I wonder now what she would have thought if she knew an Irishman brought his daughter out to see the King of England's daughter. When Daddy took my sister and brother to watch President Roosevelt's funeral procession, I was too lazy to get out of bed that early.

One of my most favorite experiences was going on my own to the Watergate to see a ballet performance. It was filled to capacity so they put folding chairs up in the very front for the late comers. From that distance I could actually smell the dancer's sweat and hear the loud steps of their soft shoes. We saw many famous entertainers at prices we could afford on a government grade three salary. I could go on and on, but the most telling thing about being a Washingtonian is we did not have the vote.

DC did not even have a vote for the president in those days. Just how unfair I realized when I heard my in-laws, who left Pennsylvania ten years before, were able to get their son's orders in the Army changed to something better by calling their congressman in Pennsylvania.

Then the great day came when we could vote for a delegate and council members. The ballot was loaded with the names to be selected for various positions. I knew none of the people; what should I do? I voted for all the women. The next day when I told my very intelligent female supervisor how I voted she feigned surprise and disappointment at my choice. Surprised at her reaction, I asked her how she voted. She had a great laugh and said, "I voted for every other one." It wasn't we were stupid about most things, just in the privilege we never knew. Even now I make myself vote in all state and local elections, try to learn about the candidates, then vote - but my heart's not in it. I feel like I never learned its importance.

To Be or Not To Be Prejudiced

I was brought up in a very tolerant Irish immigrant household. I never heard any negative comments about African Americans, nor even the English, probably because my mother worked as a ladies maid in a home with English and Scottish help, and my father was a day laborer for some years.

We lived in Northeast DC off of Montello Avenue which housed a small black community that we passed through on our way to school, church, and the stores; yet I hardly remember seeing them. They did not go to our schools although I have a photo of our Holy Communion class which shows five or six African Americans. Our church cordoned off the last three pews for them which upset my father so much he gave up his job of ushering. I think now, the arrangement was better than none. My father only had a fourth grade education but could tell by their dress that these black families were further up the ladder, professionals, so to speak. This was odd of my father as he was not too impressed by the white person's standing in the community. He looked for something more rock solid in a person than a title. I suppose he related to black people because he worked with them as a laborer and witnessed the prejudice meted out to them.

One day my mother and I came in from the front porch and found a young black girl in the dining room going through Mom's purse. She saw us and quickly turned to leave through the back porch when my mother went over to her and asked her if she needed some money. She just stood there. Mom reached in her purse and gave her some, though probably not much. My mother knew and felt what it was like to be poor.

Although we lived amidst the Afro-American community, my first encounter with a black person was one evening while dragging my sled up a snowy hill at the end of our block. There he was, a young boy my age, seven or eight years old, with very short black kinky hair. We stood and looked at each other. I reached up with my hand and felt his hair; it was so soft. We smiled, then went on with our fun.

One night my father took me to their neighborhood to see a party in progress. The house had a concrete sunken patio where everyone was dressed in evening clothes, talking and laughing to the music from a small band. It was so beautiful to me that I still remember the house as being marble and the people in it as movie stars.

Despite this upbringing, apparently somewhere deep inside, there was a germ of prejudice which I sorrowfully discovered in the fourth grade. In our Catholic school you saved pennies to buy African babies. It sounds terrible but we loved to think we were helping these children in the care of the missionaries. Sister Angela was showing us a picture of a missionary holding a child and telling us how wonderful it was to hold these children. For some unexplainable reason, I got a disgusted look on my face and probably voiced an "ugh." Sister looked at me as if she couldn't believe it. "This is God's child. We are all God's children," or words to that effect. I never forgot it. In years to come, I found myself in three different situations where the dark web of prejudice came upon me without warning, for no reason, no reason at all, but at least now I could recognize it for what it was, "Stupidity," and deal appropriately with it.

The 1930s In DC

Two or three times a day we walked through the "colored" neighborhood to go to school and church and to the stores; yet I only met one black person in 14 years.

> As I was a sledding
> I saw his kinky hair
> And stopped to look at him
> And touched his head with care.(Refrain)

I asked him where he went to school
    Way uptown with the other blacks
And where does your father work
    Way downtown on the streetcar tracks.(Refrain)

Come on up to our street
You'll like the games we play
    White girl, your mind's gone astray
    Your mind's done gone astray.(Refrain)

Refrain:
Their world was all around us
Yet we did not see nor hear
We chose to close our eyes and ears
So such a sin would not appear.

A Child's Summer in DC before Air Conditioning

AM: With your bare feet around its trunk
    And your nose flat against its bark
    You thought you felt its being
      (You were young - 6 or 7)
    You knew you felt its heart.

Then you'd drop onto the cool ground
Into the shade of this oak tree
Till the boys came out with their marbles
And played at your feet. (So long ago)

LIFE IN DC

> PM: All the windows were wide open
> The curtains tied back with a sheer
> You slept almost bare in this modest home
> Searching your bed for the slightest breeze
> At last, the sweet dreams finally come
> As you twist and turn in the damp sheets.

It Was the 50s and Early 60s

Do you remember how affordable live entertainment was before TV? I was living at home on a government clerk's salary. I remember seeing Ethel Merman in "Call Me Madam" and Carol Channing in "Gentlemen Prefer Blondes" at the Capitol Theater in downtown DC. I sat four feet away from Louis Armstrong playing at the small Blue Mirror Café on 14th Street. Jimmy Dean sang at some little dive behind Union Station. But the best was Sophie Tucker who performed on the large Charles Night Club stage in Baltimore - what a sense of humor; what a great husky laugh. She sang her heart out and there wasn't a sound from the huge audience until they clapped their hearts out.

Then TV came. Of all the best moments, I remember the night I watched Mike Wallace introduce a funny, ordinarily dressed, plain young woman. I don't remember a line from the interview, but I remember distinctly the moment she walked over to the microphone beside the grand piano. She smiled confidently and poised herself to sing; but then she changed her mind, turned from the mike, reached up to her lips, grinned while taking a wad of gum from her mouth, and parked it under the piano's open strings. Then she began to sing. She opened her mouth and my heart swelled. I remember it all so well. The hairs stood straight up on my arms and stayed that way until she finished her song. There was no audience to give her a hand but I made a point of remembering her name. Her name was Barbara Streisand. She was nineteen.

Past, Present, and Future

The good old days - were they? I think that socially they probably were, because people had more children, which meant more cousins, which meant more social activities such as christenings, wedding, and funerals. And, of course, we were younger.

But as for other comparisons, I'm sure my mother and father were glad to get a gas furnace instead of having to shovel coal and stoking the fire every day. We all liked the radio, but when the TV came along, it became the main entertainment. Although we never talked about being stifling hot in the summer, Washington DC was a sauna; we left every window in the house open until we got this wonderful gadget called a fan. You can imagine how we felt when we got air conditioning in the 60's, COLD.

As children in the city, we had more freedom. Like us, our children also enjoyed this freedom since we had a playground at the end of the street. Our grandchildren grew up in the suburbs and rarely ventured outside the neighborhood. As far as socializing, I have to remember they attended coed schools and summer camps, and they had experiences we never knew such as vacationing in the Islands and skiing in Utah. I am pleased my children had some work experience in the summer.

Certainly war has been with us the entire century; also pedophiles, but we know them now. I don't feel any peace around the corner; the A-Bomb is the big question mark. At least the fight for Civil Rights was somewhat successful. Of course immigration is the problem now, just as it was at the turn of the century. It's hard to believe my mother-in-law was educated for her first three years in a German speaking school in Erie, Pennsylvania. Now all those horrible Irish Catholics, who had trouble being hired, had grandchildren who were soon in every walk of life, and were Irish only on Saint Patrick's Day (along with all the other nationalities). I feel that is the way the Muslims will likely be in a few generations.

LIFE IN DC

As far as healthcare is concerned, I know it is better and continues to improve but it's so boring to hear and read about it ad infinitum. I don't know how most of us survived in those good old days since we never went to the doctor unless it was for a necessary operation. As for the food pyramid, I don't think I ate that much food in a week. As a child, I cried when certain vegetables were on the table. A few of our grandchildren, like me, were very picky eaters (meat and potatoes) but are now six feet or on their way. My father-in-law was a small man who was never sick even though the ten years he lived with us he had a half a can of Campbell soup in mid-morning, two Slim Jims, two shots and four beers, then a small dinner. He never ate salad, or fruit or drank fruit juices or milk. Oh, I forgot, he smoked a couple of cigars and he chewed tobacco every day. He lived to be 86, but I must admit his wife ate very healthfully and she lived to be 92.

Financially, everyone I know is doing better than in the good old days, but I think having enough to live from payday to payday worked fine for us with the help of Sears credit. Since my husband's family and my family rented most of their life, he and I greatly appreciated not only buying a home but paying it off. I realize we now have a "consumer" culture but I don't think it affected our family to any great extent, thank goodness. What everyone else does is their choice. Being a devoted Christian socialist at heart, I cannot imagine why people need mega mansions and so many shoes to be happy.

As far as sports today, I suppose the players weren't paid enough in the olden days but what they're paid now is obscene. Of course, my husband says they can only play for so long because of injuries, etc. Does it make any sense to deliberately harm your body? I once read that the preoccupation of the Romans with the Arena Sports was one of the reasons for their decline.

What can I say about TV? In the old days, TV was very family friendly. Now it is 24 hour gossip about people we don't even know.

And I must say I think it is "unchaste." I look at the screen a lot, and believe me I'm not easily shocked but surfing through it is an "eye opener" or better said an "eye closer." Of course, there are many worthwhile programs, as with books we choose what we watch. Like the books we read, it's our choice. I must admit some of my children and I love the CSIs and the NCISs. We don't seem to mind the killing as long as nobody's naked or having sex.

Then there is the drug problem. A friend of ours has a photo of her grandfather sitting in the middle of a field in Lebanon while smoking an opium pipe. My cousin in the 1940s gave her children paregoric to help them sleep soundly when they had a party. Paregoric is an opium; you didn't have to sign for it then.

As you can probably tell, I think everything is better now. I think the diversification of the people in our country is healthy. I believe in the separation of church and state, but it seems as a secular country we have lost a devoutness we once knew, or I once knew. Upon seeing photos of the Muslims prostrate, I know how good their devoutness feels and I'm pretty sure in a few generations they will lose a lot of their reverence.

The pros and cons of the Internet I leave to the next generation. I heard there is a new program that enables you to carry a small camera on your body, so you have a pictorial journal of your life. This must be as close as person can get to Narcissism. I cannot begin to imagine what will come next. All periods have wonderful inventions; it's all of us who manage to misuse them.

So, as far as the future goes, I think often about Carl Sandburg's poem "Grass" which talks about the grass covering Ypres and erasing the horror of WWI - then I came up with another stanza:

LIFE IN DC

> Maybe ten years from now, they'll look over the water
>> What place is this?
>> Where are we now?
>> I was the ice.
>> You let me melt.

Our Bamboo

In 1964 we bought a house on Rodman Street in Northwest Washington DC. It needed a lot of work but first we took down the garage. My son and I decided we wanted to spruce it up with some bamboo. A woman who was visiting our neighbors cautioned us. She said we would be very, very sorry.

Now these were not the small Japanese type you read poems about.

> Against his will, my husband planted them
> In the backyard, next to the patio
> Tall stalks of bamboo that grew inches every day
> They said that we'd regret that deed,
> Indeed we did, but what a show!

> The wispy green leaves whispering to the oak
> Bowing to the wind, kneeling in the snow
> All the time, reaching round and round beneath the ground
> Shooting in and out and over the retaining wall
> Piercing the lily pond and without a sound
> BURSTING through the concrete floor

> They said we'd regret that deed and they were right
> But what a sight! What a treat!
> Watching the bamboo grow on Rodman Street
> In Northwest Washington DC.

We Human Beings

We're a social lot
We human beings
But we're solitary
More lonely than we like to admit
Always seeking out our roots
Questioning our future
Yearning for answers
To why we're here.

Why <u>are</u> we here on this magical planet?
Are we HIS experiment to create the perfect Soul
And then what form will *they* become
Those who'll be combing through our bones
20,000 years from now, down among our catacombs
Gazing in wonder at our thumbs.

(*I'm assuming they'll only need a few fingers to control their robots.*)

Out of the Mouths of Babes

Fortunately, I have no heart breaking experiences to recall. Either I have lived a charmed life or I choose not to remember (or most likely) I won't allow it to happen.

But I had a few experiences that brought forth such tender emotions I would call "heart rending." Some years ago on a visit to my daughter's home, I sat at the dining room table between my autistic grandson, Matija, age 8 and his cousin, Tessa, age 4. As he didn't speak, I attempted to encourage him to speak by asking him to say "Yes" when I offered him the ice cream we were having for dessert. "Matija, just say, Yes," and I would nod my head at the same time. There were no words from Matija. After two or three times with no response I felt this little hand on my arm. I looked down at my little grandchild; Tessa looked up at me with these pleading eyes and said with the wisdom of Solomon, "Granma, Matija wants some ice cream, he says Yes." My heart trembled at such understanding.

A few years later when Matija was about ten, I was watching him at the swimming pool when two or three boys started to make fun of him. At this age he was talking but in an unusual and loud manner. Before I could reach them, a young boy, maybe 8 years of age, walked hurriedly through the water toward them and shouted "Stop. Stop it," he said, "Can't you see, he's a special child." I thought my heart would break. What courage, what compassion from one so young. It was truly heart rending.

God's Entertainment Box
(after reading Sir Walter Raleigh "On the Life of Man")

Just what is our part
In this, His Grand Scheme--
Actors He Twitters
On Facebook, U-Tube,
And MySpace dot com?

Does the Majestic Scanner
Click on our icon--
Watch us freely love,
Kill, steal, and kneel
While He Jumps with Joy
      Stoops in Sorrow
        Laughs Out Loud?

Are we his paperbacks--
Mysteries to solve
Or a movie to browse
Till He can bear no more--
Then moves the golden mouse?

When our role is played
And we zoom onto His scene
Will we be a floppy disc or a single file
Or just a pixel on another screen?

Or are we recycled?
Or do we just crash?
Or will we be on His Website--At Last.

LIFE IN DC

An Irish Mist

They call it a soft rain
It doesn't even drizzle
You can taste it on your lips
But you really can't feel it

It's not a rain at all
It's a stranger to the ground
It's like a mist ……… a kiss
……… a whisper of a sound

◆ ◆ ◆ ◆ ◆

About the Author

Anne Doherty Rinn was born (1930) in Washington DC of Irish parents. She attended Holy Name (grade school) and Notre Dame Academy (high school). During her professional career she worked at PEPCO, LUTC, and for the United States Government.

She married her husband Raymond (Pat) in 1958. They have five children and eight grandchildren. They retired to Delaware at age 55 where they did volunteer work for 11 years, then moved to Olney for 10 years, then to Leisure World for the next 12 years.

CHAPTER 15

Reality and Beyond

By Bobbie Troy

We Need to Believe [1]

we need to believe
in something
that we cannot touch
or feel emotionally
something within
or without
that is beyond seeing
beyond doubt
because sometimes
what we have
just isn't enough

---

[1] Originally published 3/26/18:
https://cavalcadeofstars.wordpress.com/2018/03/26/bobbie-troy-20/

I Speak to You [2]

I speak to you
not from the grave
but from the air
around you
the sun above
and the ground under your feet

I speak to you
as one who cherished
your love and friendship
shared with you joy and pain
and moved through life
feeling better
for knowing each other

I speak to you
not as a subscriber
to any belief of an afterlife
but to good memories
of all we were to each other
and all we were meant to be

I speak to you
as family and friend
and wish
that we may share
another moment together
somewhere between
being and nothingness

---

[2] Originally published 6/4/18:
https://cavalcadeofstars.wordpress.com/2018/06/04/bobbie-troy-22/

Dear Diane [3]

if you remember
i think it was in some strange court in tasmania
or maybe in your kitchen/our kitchen over coffee
that you took out your precious written thoughts

and pushed the sugar my way

if you remember
i think it was in your kitchen/our kitchen in the
   afternoon sunlight
that you let me see the back of your head/heart
and the reasons behind, the contacts with
all the things that didn't let you be free

and I got up to get the milk from the frig

if you remember
i think it was in the middle of a fresh pot of coffee
after so many cups of instant
that we realized where we were in terms of each other
and what we were

and sometime during all that
you gave me a new coffee mug

---

[3] Originally published December 2009 on www.voxpoetic.com. Nominated by Annmarie Lockhart, editor, for the 2010 Pushcart Prize.

The Door of Life [4]

I stood in front of an abyss
with fragility on my left
uncertainty on my right
and a fall into blackness
in front of me
not wanting to choose
any of them
I turned around
to go back to my former life
but found that the door
through which I came
was closed

Reality Heals Itself [5]

like the cry
of a lone wolf
reality comes home
to routine
and occasional rapture
while the molecules
of everyday life
settle and fill
the wounds
allowing reality
to heal itself

---

[4] Originally published 7/7/12: http://thecamelsaloon.blogspot.com/2012/07/door-of-life.html
[5] Originally published 3/8/12: http://thecamelsaloon.blogspot.com/2012/03/reality-heals-itself.html

Surviving Auschwitz [6]

when the guards removed my clothes
they thought they took my soul
but I managed to hide it
in an invisible pocket

when night came
I retrieved my soul
from its hiding place
and used it like a blanket
to cover
my naked, starving, dying body

Beyond Tomorrow [7]

if I could see
beyond tomorrow
I would collect
my laughter
in a jar
and save it
for those dark days
(you know the ones)

---

[6] Originally published 11/11/2010, the 72nd anniversary of Kristallnacht: http://voxpoetica.com/surviving-auschwitz/
[7] Originally published 5/10/16: http://voxpoetica.com/tomorrow-2/

Answers [8]

there are no answers
only people who think
they have answers

The Greatest Lesson [9]

i long to understand
the precious filaments
of the firmament
and how they affect me
this speck of nothingness
on a lone planet
but the greatest lesson
i have learned
is not to look up
or outward
but only inward
finding that i am one
of the precious filaments

---

[8] Originally published 8/24/12: http://voxpoetica.com/two-by-bobbie-troy/
[9] Originally published 8/24/12: http://voxpoetica.com/two-by-bobbie-troy/

Layers of Time [10]

layers of time
lash across my body
like a winter wind
pushing
relentless
unforgiving
as if I deserved
a punishment
for aging

The Fallen [11]

they are falling
all around me
like soldiers in battle

but they are not soldiers
they are my friends,
friends of friends,
family, and friends of family
each at the end of their life
but winning no medals
for being heroes in their time
for being strong enough to get through life
facing whatever they had to face

they are falling
all around me
like soldiers in battle

---

[10] Originally published 9/10/18: http://voxpoetica.com/layers-of-time/
[11] Originally published 7/14/18: http://voxpoetica.com/the-fallen/

She: Losing the Plot [12]

i knew
long before the rest
before she started floating
and swirling through each day
that the connections
were being interrupted
the drugs had finally
taken their toll
she was losing the plot
and there was nothing
i could do

My Mind Is Free [13]

unlike my body
that is tethered to the ground
by gravity
my mind is free

unlike my heart
that is wrapped around yours
my mind is free

unlike the minions
of guilt and remorse
on my doorstep
my mind is free

but where is the freedom
that I am supposed to feel?

---

[12] Originally published 3/26/18: https://cavalcadeofstars.wordpress.com/2018/03/26/bobbie-troy-20/
[13] Originally published 2/13/12: http://cavalcadeofstars.wordpress.com/

Emptiness

I remember walking on the beach
in the late afternoon sun
you smiled and I knew
it was the perfect moment
to pop the question

now, as I sit alone
at the breakfast table
thinking about those last days
of chemo treatments
that made you so sick
I wonder how I can survive
walking on the beach alone

♦ ♦ ♦ ♦ ♦

About the Author

Bobbie Troy maintains sanity and perspective on life by writing poetry, flash fiction, and original fairy tales with a 21st century twist. Within the Writers Group of Leisure World, she is known for her poetry. Her work is published widely online and in some print anthologies. Her poem, "Dear Diane," was nominated for a 2010 Pushcart Prize; her fairy-tale play, *Sasha and the Tree of Sorrows*, was produced in March 2011; and her poem, "Dear Diane (Letter 2)," was nominated for the 2012 Best of the Net. Bobbie also served on the Editorial Board for three anthologies. As a latecomer to the published author scene, Bobbie is proud of the fact that her first poem was published at the age of 62.

After retiring from a career in technical editing, Bobbie moved to Leisure World with her husband Sol in 2014. Writers Group of Leisure

World is a pivotal group in Bobbie's life in the community. The group provides intellectual stimulation, the opportunity to share her creative writing with friends, and socializing after the meetings.

Made in the USA
Middletown, DE
26 March 2024